2014 WORLD JOURNALS

2014 WORLD JOURNALS

Barbara Wolf & Margaret Anderson

authorHOUSE®

AuthorHouse™
1663 Liberty Drive
Bloomington, IN 47403
www.authorhouse.com
Phone: 1-800-839-8640

Published by AuthorHouse   12/04/2014

ISBN: 978-1-4969-5700-9 (sc)
ISBN: 978-1-4969-5699-6 (e)

Library of Congress Control Number: 2014921544

DEDICATED

This book is dedicated to Barbara's husband
Jack and to the rest of the world.

SPECIAL TRIBUTE TO DR. MASARU EMOTO

From Barbara:

Special tribute to water scientist Dr. Masaru Emoto who died last month on October 17, 2014.

We have known each other since I met him years ago at The Hague Appeal for Peace Conference in the Netherlands. I was in charge of putting a peace pole at the Congress Center where thousands gathered to put their minds into finding ways to stop wars. The motive was to create a culture of peace for the 21st Century that would replace the bloodiest century in history, the 20th Century.

At the Congress Center, I found a satisfactory place for the peace pole just outside the entrance to a meditation room. Irene van Schagen of The Netherlands was in charge of this meditation room. She and her husband Marco said they would petition The Hague city fathers to have the peace pole planted in front of the Peace Palace. I said, if the city fathers agree to the planting, I will return to plant the peace pole.

Within a short time, the city fathers agreed and I did return for the peace pole planting. The above is background and a bit of a digression from what I want to tell you.

During the conference, Irene van Schagen wanted a gathering of some conference attendees at her house. She asked me to choose who to invite and to invite them.

I knew no one at the congress meeting. Yet, quickly I became friends with some. One of them was Professor Hideo Nakazawa of Japan who agreed to come to an evening of talk at Irene's house. I pointed to a man sitting nearby, saying I do not know this man but I think he would be a good one to invite. Professor Nakazawa said I was looking at Dr. Masaru Emoto whom he knew very well. And so, yes, Dr. Emoto was invited. He came and sat around the table with us to talk and we all had a wonderful time together.

I quickly learned that Dr. Emoto's passion was water. He had a laboratory in Japan and he did a lot of testing. In 2004, when I was in Tokyo with Margaret Anderson and Native American SilverStar, we were invited to Dr. Emoto's office. Here we listened while Dr. Emoto explained his testing of the water. I assumed that some of this testing had to do with water consciousness and I was surprised when Dr. Emoto told me he had not yet successfully tested to a point where he could be assured that water has a consciousness. However, it did not take long for him to be reassured of water consciousness. Today he is world famous for his knowledge.

In my household, water is filtered and put in a jug before drinking. On the jug rests photographs of perfect molecular water structure coming from Dr. Emoto. Because water has a consciousness, I can expect that my filtered water will be influenced by perfect water structure coming from the photographs.

My thought is that Dr. Emoto has ascended ahead of us and he will be waiting for us. In the meantime, let us all drink healthy water. That would please him.

ACKNOWLEDGEMENTS

Chief Golden Light Eagle, Lakota Nation.
Grandmother SilverStar, Cherokee/Lakota Nation.
Patricia Cota-Robles and musician son. Musical Rapture.
Gentle Bear, Richard du Fort.
Mike and Ruth Ssembiro, Uganda.
Braco, Croatia.
Hideo Nakazawa, Japan.
Carmen Balhestero, São Paulo, Brazil.
Salwa Zeidan, Abu Dhabi, United Arab Emirates.

FOREWORD

We firmly believe in what we believe, and we realize you may not agree with everything we believe. Probably we would not agree with everything you agree with. But, let us put aside our differences and let us be friends.

It's the world that matters. Mother Earth needs help and we are trying to give it to her. That is all that is expected.

INTRODUCTION

We have put Chief Golden Light Eagle's photograph with us on the cover because he has given us important knowledge to help the world and we are grateful. This book in your hands tells you about our world travels to help.

We begin by giving you our experiences when we went to California specifically to help the dolphins and the whales. They had been sending up red flags seeking the attention of humanity because they wanted to call attention to the waters of their homeland polluted with radiation, plastic, and garbage.

Soon after California, we flew to Africa because Mother Earth had been doing a lot of rumbling. Was the Great Rift starting north and running to nearly mid-Africa a potential shift problem? We flew to Uganda to reach the rift area, and while we were there, we helped open a small school. Then we flew to the Middle East to see this place.

In March, the United Nations in New York City was on the agenda. Annually, at the Equinox, a peace bell is rung at the UN and we support this. In June, we saw Braco whose healing gaze is being seen by millions. In September, we were in Nashville, Tennessee, and then in Niagara Falls to attend Native American conferences. We attended another in Colorado in November.

Yes, 2014 was a busy year. We want to give you our experiences.

CONTENTS

CHAPTER 1

PACIFIC OCEAN CALIFORNIA

Joint Journals:

We are ready to go to the Pacific. Why?

January 18, 7 a.m.:

Barbara hears the call of the whales to come immediately to the Pacific. Margaret channels the whales and dolphins asking for advice.

Margaret Channeling:

Dear Dolphins and Whales of the Pacific, we know you are suffering because of lack of oxygen in the water. Many gathered in November to alert humanity to the danger of life forms in the Pacific due to the Fukushima radiation and other pollution in the ocean. We want to help. Should we go to Monterey Bay, California, to be on site or should we do the meditations here on the Niagara Escarpment where we live?

The Whales answer: *Go to the Bay.*

Why?

You will know our environment better first hand. Announce your arrival. We are waiting for you to come.

The Niagara Escarpment, the ancient sea of the past, is alive and awake. It is life power for the Pacific. Use this ancient sea power which comes from the origins of the planet to clear the water. Place the vibration of the ancient sea power on the Pacific that is engulfed with man-made pollution, radiation, trash, tsunami debris.

Life in the Pacific Ocean cannot be sustained. Make it a sound-free health zone so only natural sound can be picked up. Healing sound. Not loud, harsh sounds or other sounds that do not hold the best intent for preserving life forms.

Our hearing bodies are as sensitive as a newborn human baby. We are large but we are sensitive to all sound and frequencies. We are the Guardians of the Oceans. Respect us. Honor us. We are here for you, humanity! Wake up.

Treat your Brothers and Sisters of the Sea with kindness and respect. What you send out comes back. Let it be love. Let it be hope. Let it be healing. Then Planet Earth will thrive and not go staggering as it is now. What happens to the Whales and Dolphins happens to the humans. Choose wisely so that all Life thrives.

We also would be pleased that you use the Vortexes to bring powerful energy to our homeland, the oceans.

From Barbara:

We quickly prepare to fly to California and we are soon ready. But now we have a surprise. When we phone our taxi driver Mr. Dependable to take us to the airport, he says the weather is TERRIBLE, especially in Philadelphia, our first destination. Flights have been cancelled.

OH!!!

We already have printed out our boarding passes from the Internet, and when we did this, there was no indication that our flight would be cancelled.

We phone AAA which has arranged our flight and we are told that alternate ways will be checked. Within fifteen minutes, an alternative is arranged and we need to pay no more.

Hurray!!! We will be on our way tomorrow!

January 22:

Mr. Dependable picks us up and takes us to the airport for a flight to Chicago, a few hours later than we originally expected to leave. Never mind. We are on our way.

The flight is uneventful, and when we arrive at Chicago's O'Hare Airport, we are happy to see that it is not snowing, although the temperature is very, very cold. Below zero Fahrenheit. If our plane leaves, that is all that matters to us.

O'Hare has many customers today. Many! The flight board tells us which gate will be hosting our flight to San Francisco, and we must RUSH to that gate! It is far away and we begin racing at top speed to reach our destination. No carts transporting people are in sight. When we arrive, out of breath, we join passengers boarding and we are soon on the plane. Wow! That was close!

I sit at the window looking out as the pilot begins our flight to San Francisco. All below is white with snow. And then the pilot takes us above the clouds and we go along for a while with nothing visible except clouds below us. When I see a patch of white Midwest farmland, it looks bleak down there. I begin seeing miles and miles and miles of barren land. Then barren, brown mountains. News reports have been telling us there is a serious drought down there. I see no water.

A woman tells me she remembers California when water was so scarce that in order to conserve it, there was a need to flush toilets only occasionally. That was twenty years ago. The population has increased tremendously. What will happen if the drought continues?

When we arrive at the San Francisco Airport, we are surprised at the lack of customers, the opposite of what we encountered at Chicago's O'Hare. We search for an Information Desk to suggest a hotel for the night and when we have one, we take a free shuttle to the hotel, register and go to bed. Tired!

January 23, 3:00 a.m., Margaret channels:

Thank you, dear Whales and Dolphins of the Pacific for your guidance and your smoothing and clearing of obstructions for our travel.

Whale response: Obstructions clear if you drop your fear and anxiety. Be like a cork and float on the surface of events and possibilities. Fear contracts and closes possible channels and one sinks into oblivion, chaos, density, confusion, negativity.

Stay afloat on the surface. Ride the waves. Go a long distance with us whales who are travelers, sounders, balancers. We are givers and guardians of the world oceans. Note that our spine and rib cage is heart shaped.

You came to San Francisco under our guidance, the Admirals of the water. You looked for the first class whale lounge at the airport and you found the Admirals Lounge. Your membership is the Whale Dolphin Sea membership of the heart.

Your sea mission, you are getting it slowly. You need to clean the seaweed of your thoughts in order to realize you need to make a Ring of Light, Beacons of Love, Light, and Power along the Monterey Bay coastline to above San Francisco.

In a dream you saw a lady in a sari put down a framework for the DEEP, Dolphin Triangle Project, and this framework has expanded to include the entire project you are working on now. This is to balance the world's oceans on a high level.

The Monterey Bay Canyon is a peace zone, power zone for the light ring you are making. Also a Vortex Light ring.

You are making a line of beacons from one spot outwards to counteract the negativity of Fukushima radiation, tsunami debris and all trash affronts to the oceans. Would you put poison in your drinking water? That is what you are doing to ours. If the oceans go down in life force, then the planet's ability to sustain life on land goes down. Pollution in the land, pollution in the air. Go live in a chimney hut and breathe in soot. We are your brothers and sisters, your older brothers and sisters who guard your shorelines. Take away our guarding guidance and you have nothing to counteract your ignorance of spoiling the environment of the planet, the air, the water, the land and the spirit of life force of Mother Earth.

Come swim with us with your hearts. Love is the guidance. Track us with Love intent. We will open the world for you. We have waited for this rendezvous.

Today, Margaret, you cannot physically enter the water because it is too cold, too rough for you, but you can enter the water via the heart mind of love intent. Distances do not exist nor does the cold or the hot. All is just right with the heart mind of love intent.

Come, come, come to the ocean, the Pacific Ocean, into the deep canyon, the center point, and then spread outward love to the whole Pacific. You were in California earlier but focused on the land, not the sea. Now the sea dominates and you need to understand the importance of the whales and dolphins for the preservation of the life force of the oceans. Expand your love. Expand your light.

Come into our waters. Hear our song. Follow us as we travel north. Follow us as we travel in all dimensions. Follow us heart to heart. Open and show yourself. Call out your love to us. Striving and pushing too hard gets one stopped at the beginning. Be cool and use the smooth love frequency of Movement and Balance, our symbol, to deliver your letter of thought to us. We are here in your office (hotel bathroom) dictating our letter. Smile. This is funny. Whales and the dolphins have a great sense of humor. Humans have lower levels of humor. The bird cocks its head for a better angle and the whale cocks its mind/sonar direction for a better angle of awareness. You are in our angle of awareness. We are in your angle of awareness.

Awareness Lounge, First Class. That is your travel membership to our world here. Welcome, welcome, welcome. You were already here before you started.

Love and cosmic greetings from the Whales of Planet Earth. Swim in the curl of the wave, not future, not past. We will give you codings for Mother Earth.

I ask: What are codings?

Answer: Information for enhancing, growing, understanding life. Codings can be used for knowledge, for a state of being, being-ness. They can affect the atomic molecular structure of things. Codings can affect the whole planet, the orbit, the solar system, the universe, the universes.

Vortex codings have been given to you as symbols to be transported from place to place and put down with love intent for healing the planet. Codings are transparent to the right person and not transparent to another. They are apparent in plain sight, but invisible to others. Use the codings for healing the oceans. Use them for timing and mechanism enhancement, and enhancement of growth. Use them for coming together, for breaking down barriers, for unifying the whole.

Whale codings encompass all. They are heard, seen, felt through Love. Whale codings are Light frequencies. They can stop a storm, balance earth plates. We are moving, sounding machines sending out balancing modalities for the planet -- oceans and land. You cannot separate the two. We continue night and day. Part of us sleeps; part of us continues.

We work brain to brain. Our thoughts spout out like our spouting of water. Ideas go out. Codings go out. Be a receiver of whale codes. Whale codes are all around you. You pick up what is on your frequency. If all people could turn and pause from their hurried lives and receive these codings of love and balance and dynamic wisdom, the planet's scars would be healed and ceaseless fighting would cease.

The New Golden Age of oceans and land on earth would be here if warring factions swam with us and began to learn how precious life is, how precious is cooperation with the whole, with the inner guidance of each individual with inner balance. Then all is in harmony. Then the individual and society would thrive. The New Golden Age of the oceans and land on Earth would be here.

January 23, from Barbara:

This morning when both of us are awake, we begin our day leisurely, talking about the channeling of the dolphins and whales. We would like to spend the morning discussing this, but because we have arrived late in California we have lost time doing work we planned to do here. And so, we pack our nightclothes and have our suitcases ready when a shuttle from the hotel will return us to the airport. However, we stay long enough to have a good breakfast of waffles. Who knows when we will have time to eat again.

At the airport, we rent a medium-sized car and then begin tackling SF traffic. This city is BIG! One does not realize how many cars are on the city streets until one begins driving. We move along smoothly going south with our minds on Santa Cruz because we know we only have to go a bit further to reach Aptos, location of the Rio Sands Hotel where we should have stayed last night.

When we reach the hotel, a pleasant surprise greets us. Front desk receptionists wearing friendly smiles tell us we have been given a free cancellation for last night's room. They have taken pity on us because of the awful weather performance to the East. Also, they have even extended our reservation for a couple more nights. We are happy.

We are soon at the nearby beach, not only feeling happy for the friendly hotel people being so kind to us, but also we are happy that the friendly Pacific is right here in front of us, showing us a warm friendly personality.

Margaret begins carving Vortexes in the sand at the water's edge. These Vortex symbols have been given to humanity as a gift to the planet via Chief Golden Light Eagle and Grandmother SilverStar. Our work is to place their powerful energy around the world to help Mother Earth and all who live on her.

The two Native Americans have spent years bringing in this 'off world' information. At the back of our book is a Glossary explaining symbols and Vortexes. Also in the Glossary is an explanation of sacred music called Musical Rapture, A Healing Gift for Humanity. We use this music with our work.

While Margaret is placing the Vortexes on the sand, I am playing the sacred music to bring in singing from the Angelic Kingdom. This singing comes from a higher dimension than the third. When the two dimensions meet, this is Zero Point. I put my energy field at Zero Point and send out thoughts that I want the water to be healed. In the Middle Ages, if done correctly, lead could have been turned into gold. Because I want the water to be healed, I work in this manner while Margaret is drawing symbols by the ocean and encircling each for activation.

Margaret speaks to the ocean as she puts down the Vortexes. She draws symbols for the Vortex of Symmetry and the Vortexes of Strength, Health and Happiness and Right Relationship. The ocean comes in and takes the symbols immediately. She draws more and a great wave comes in and takes them all. Then she puts down the symbols of Love and Healing and the ocean keeps them on the sand as a gift to humanity and all who live on Mother Earth. A seagull watches intently.

Margaret's channeling from the whales tells her to use the energies of the Niagara Escarpment to bring power to the ocean. At one time the Niagara Escarpment was once the bottom of the ocean when negativity was not on this planet. Therefore, the remains of the escarpment consist of positive energy. We overlay this energy on the water. Also, we sprinkle sacred healing Agnihotra ash on the water to counter radiation. At the same time, we are using our minds to put this ash over all the waters of the world.

A seal appears to acknowledge the Vortex gift and Margaret wonders if this seal is a relative or friend of the blind seal living in an aquarium in Galveston, Texas. The blind seal was originally from San Francisco harbor.

A flock of ducks swim by and pause near the Vortex area. We think they can feel the energy that just has been put into the ocean here. Sea gulls fly overhead.

Then a depressed young man walks by and walks over the traces of the Vortexes. His manner appears to be close to one who would commit suicide. We give him intense love.

We spend a long time here at the ocean. When the sun begins to set, it brings intense colors of gold and shimmering green on the water. Margaret says she sees the water become the sea life of birds and fish. We feel the consciousness of whales and dolphins and we send love to the Sea Consciousness as a whole. Margaret is in tears.

When we return to the hotel, we phone Grandmother SilverStar to report the events of the day and the gifting of the Vortexes. She sings a sacred water song for us and we send it out to the ocean.

We go to bed early because we are tired, but before 9:00 p.m. we are awake. Our minds are on the trip tomorrow. We need to go to Moss Landing located at a place where the ocean floor becomes a canyon that goes down twelve thousand feet, like the Grand Canyon. Here, in the deep canyon of Moss Landing, whales and other sea life find abundant food. But now their food, small fish, are dying. Whales and other mammals who eat them will have a diminished food chain to rely on. How can whales survive?

We also know that radiation from Fukushima is killing sea life, and this diminishes the food chain. How can we stop radiation? Margaret and I ponder on this and we realize that sunlight on water can be a technique. We can use neutrinos from the sun to turn the radiation into the energy of love.

Margaret channels, calling to the dolphins and whales for help.

The response: Work with the sunlight on water, neutrinos on the surface and below the surface. Sunlight on water is a key. In plain sight. Command particles with love for the higher good. Focus on neutrinos dealing with dispersing of radiation.

Lift your mind out of the box and place the radiation frequency in a separate holding dimension. Sound can change frequency. Command by love.

January 24, from Barbara:

The day arrives after a rough night! We have breakfast before driving to Moss Landing harbor at the mouth of a deep ocean canyon. When we arrive at Moss Landing Beach State Park, we leave the car to begin climbing a big sand dune as tall as a three or four-storey building. Walking is hard because the sand is soft. When we reach the top and go down the other side, we walk to the coarse hard sand near the ocean's edge. The weather is cloudy. Good! Rain may be coming. California needs it desperately. We walk to the water's edge, noting how far the high tides have come in.

Older surfers are here with their shiny wetsuits and surfboards. One surfer is young, around 16, who is an avid surfer. We speak to him and he tells us he swims with the sea otters and dolphins. He likes this and they greet him and swim with him. He says they enjoy being with the surfers. We love what he is saying because we understand that here is one human who joins with the ocean and sea creatures so that the three become one.

From Margaret:

I take off my shoes and socks, roll up my pants, and head to the water to draw the Vortexes. To my surprise, a seal pops his head out of the water. My heart leaps up. He knew we were coming with the Vortexes!!! Amazing!!

The sand is hard, excellent for carving. The ocean, quite misty, is attentive. I draw the Symbols of the Vortex of Light, Sound and Vibration, the Vortex of Integrity, and the Vortex of Symmetry. Then, a BIG WAVE comes and takes all the symbols. I run and do not get caught by the wave.

I draw eight more symbols along the beach, and when I am ready to draw the Symbol of Future Sight, an amazing thing happens. Here in the sand at the very spot I am to draw the symbol is a curved brown sea grass in the form of the symbol! ASTOUNDING! How is that possible? A divine coincidence? I feel a divine smile coming from the Higher Worlds.

From Barbara:

I begin playing the sacred Musical Rapture and joining this energy with the Niagara Escarpment positive energy to give to the ocean in front of me.

About fifty yards away, a flock of about 100 water birds are seated on the shore near the water. They are resting, not eating. As Margaret begins putting down the vortexes, they become curious and one flies toward us to investigate. I tell him to bring his flock and come to sit in the energies of the vortexes. He returns to his flock and two more birds come to investigate.

Now I am addressing the entire flock with my thoughts -- come, come, come. And yes, they do come. They do not fly. They stay on the land at the water's edge and scurry toward us. Then they stop for a moment before scurrying again. I continue addressing my thoughts to them. Come, come, come.

They come. They stay. They stay until Margaret has finished putting down the vortexes and she is sitting on the sand with me. Then they investigate the sand where she has drawn the vortexes. They peck. We know they are pecking at the energy that has been put down.

It would be easy to sit all day at this wonderful Moss Landing beach but we must set our sights on reaching the city of Monterey to visit the famous Monterey Bay Aquarium with its mighty display of ocean life.

When we do reach the area, this is a busy dot on our California map, and we are happy there are many signs showing us the way to the aquarium. Fortunately, when we are arriving, our eyes land on a nearby parking lot where we can leave our rental car while we amble through the aquarium. We know there is much to see. And yes, there is much to see!

We begin by standing at a balcony railing overlooking the Pacific. Later, Margaret will place the vortexes on this railing for the Pacific and the sea creatures inside the aquarium.

We are impressed by the staff eager to help visitors. When we ask about programs in the auditorium, we are shown a listing of performances and we are personally directed there. A film of deep sea life is ready to begin and we take seats to watch. Now we are shown an amazing fact: there are dots of light in the dark parts of the water. These are actually sea creatures!

When the film is over, we learn it is time to feed sea otters and we walk to the exhibit that holds a rescued baby sea otter found abandoned at a shoreline. This baby is with another baby sea otter and both are being fed by two aquarium assistants holding buckets of food for them. The system of feeding is to throw the food toward the mouths of the two otters who then grab the food and quickly devour it. I do not know whether or not this new baby will be returned to the ocean, but I do see the delight of the assistants as the baby is responding beautifully.

From Margaret:

After we see the film, Mysteries of the Deep, we tour the aquarium and enjoy the kelp exhibit, the touching pools, the sea bird habitat, the sea skates, the small schools of fish, the feeding of otters. We see egrets, cormorants, all sorts of water birds, and pelicans. It is an overwhelming place.

While we are having lunch here, we see people gathered at the viewing deck and I run out to check. They have seen a gray whale going south!! It does not surface again, but I know the whale has passed through the energy field of the Vortexes.

When we leave the aquarium and I walk to a nearby beach to draw the Vortexes, I cannot reach the beach because harbor seals are resting on it. I do not want to disturb the happy sunbathers so I return to the aquarium to draw the Vortexes on the balcony railing. They make a Beacon of Light for Monterey Bay.

When I finish, we now have Beacons of Light at three places – Aptos, Moss Landing and Monterey Bay.

We feel good about this. We have done our best. Tomorrow we will turn our faces northward. We drive back to the hotel, eat, and go to bed early. Tired.

January 25, 5:00 a.m., Margaret Channeling:

Dear Whales and Dolphins, I want to tell you that yesterday we placed three Beacons of Light at the Pacific.

Their response: Dear Margaret, you have a blank canvas to use as you wish. We are aware of you putting down the Beacons of Light. Place them at Santa Cruz and continue going north. You are fully connected with the Pacific. You have established a point and you spread outward your love, your light. The Vortexes bring the Power. Keep on.

There are awake humans and asleep humans. Look at the man caught in his depression who almost walked into you.

Sing your song as the birds sing their song to wake up the plants and growing things to clean the environment, to bring in the sun. Sing your song to greet the new day, to give love to the oceans and humanity. When the ocean is honored, loved, then the frequencies change and the land is softened, the weather becomes more moderate.

Look for harmony in Nature. It is all around – the flowers, the trees, the birds, the sea creatures, the stones, the shells, all great teachers.

Enjoy the Day. Spread Love and Light this day. Peace, Love and Light this day. Bring on the Beacons.

Our blessings for today from the Pacific World Cosmic Whales and Dolphins.

Barbara remarks:

At breakfast we eat and check out of the hotel and go briefly to the nearby ocean before travelling up the coast to Santa Cruz Municipal Wharf to see a big population of sea lions. It is easy enough to drive to Santa Cruz, but finding the wharf, home of many sea lions, is another matter. We expect to find signs pointing the way, but we see no signs. Maybe everyone is aware of how to reach the wharf and so there is no need for signs. Well, a stop three or four times to ask direction results in our finding the wharf which extends a long way. We drive to the very end where we park the car to see a group of about twenty to thirty young sea lions swimming round-and-round in a tight pod. They are just off the end of the wharf and it is wonderful to be so close to them.

We hear loud snorting and barks, and we poke our heads over the wharf railing to look down about ten feet to see two large sea lions stretched out on a wooden structure. They are nose to nose, snuffling each other as they sleep. The wharf pilings are narrow where they sleep and make their homes. How can they be comfortable? I think the city should widen a bit their narrow homes.

Margaret Journal:

I see adult clusters of sea lions and baby clusters of sea lions. Then I see a snuggling pair of sea lions, nose to nose, asleep on the railing below me and I begin singing to this loving couple Fred Astaire's song, 'Dancing Cheek to Cheek'. They are so sweet, so happy.

I begin drawing the Vortexes on the railing here, and when I draw the Universal Law of Life, the sea lions bark. Another Beacon of Light has been lit!

We phone SilverStar, and when she answers, we tell her to click on her computer Internet source to hear sea lions barking. She does!! She hears them barking. Success!!

Barbara Journal:

We linger here a bit, reluctant to leave this wonderful place, but we have a distance to go. We say good-bye to the sea lions and begin driving slowly off the long wharf to the land roads. Our destination is North with no definite stop on our minds. We need to find a good place to put down another Beacon of Light for the Pacific.

We drive on Route 1 and we reach a place called Pacifica Beach. This beach beckons to us and we know it will be a good place to stop. Very quickly we see a big hotel, Victorian style, called the Pacifica Beach Hotel. Yes, we will stay here if there is a room for us. It is Saturday, the weekend, and so maybe there will be no vacancy.

Success! Two rooms are available and we take the one at the top of the hotel complex. This means driving smartly up a road toward the sky, and when we do reach our destination, we are happy. After we unlock the door of our room and we find a big Jacuzzi taking up nearly a third of available space, we are delighted. Probably we will not use it, but we are amused to have it in the room. Whoever heard of such a thing? Are there many California hotel rooms with Jacuzzis?

January 26, Sunday:

When we wake, we know it will be a perfect day to be at Pacifica Beach. Surfers will be playing with surf here. We are at the beach before 9 a.m. and this Sunday the parking lot is already filling up. One has to pay to park here. We have to put three dollars in a machine that will automatically give us a ticket for parking for four hours. Before we put our money in the machine, we watch two tall, thin, well-conditioned male surfers trying to make the machine give them a ticket after they have inserted a credit card. For a reason they do not understand, the machine refuses, and so they must revert to using cash. We ask them to help us get a ticket, and they are obliging, helpful, friendly. We have been noting that Californians are friendly and helpful.

Already, about twenty-five surfers are in the water, most patiently waiting to for a good wave for them to play with. We sit for a time watching them before Margaret begins drawing the vortexes on the sand. I play the sacred Musical Rapture and connect this to the Niagara Escarpment, to the Pacific Ocean, to all the waters of the world.

I feel the Pacific is happy today. Its consciousness is available for all who can connect. And yes, the Pacific loves the surfers who are here at Pacifica Beach playing with its surf.

We are in no rush to leave this wonderful beach with all its surfers in the water. We linger here enjoying the site. Tomorrow we will be on the plane taking us East and we will be seeing no more surfers. Yes, we linger here, reluctant to leave.

Yet, we know there is work to do. We must make our way to the Golden Gate Bridge and cross it in order to drive to Stinson Beach where we will place another Beacon of Light.

Margaret Journal:

At Pacifica Beach I enjoy watching the surfers and the waves. I think of the dolphins and sea creatures.

I channel to whomever wants to speak:

The seals speak: We are here with the humans to share water. We can feel when humans project love to us. We bask in the sun. We bask in love. Our hearts are very sensitive and we connect easily heart to heart with the human. Remember, Margaret, your encounter with the seal at the National Zoo in Washington, DC when you wept with your love of the seal who kept going round and round close to the glass looking directly at you – soul to soul. Remember the blind seal from San Francisco living in the Galveston aquarium who received the codings from Giza and danced and sent out the codings to us the seals of the world. The seal consciousness is close to you. It is accessed through the Love Channel -- almost magnetic -- eye to eye -- heart to heart.

The sea lions join in: We thrive in a group. We receive warmth and protection from a group. We bask in the sun in a group, some in the water, some out of the water, always on alert, the 'resters' knowing the watchers are on duty. The small sea lions swim in a cluster for unity of the group. Facile swimmers swim the outer circle.

We sea lions are massive. The seals are more delicate. We sea lions love that you came to our home you call the Wharf near Santa Cruz, the plank structure where we live and feed and grow our young.

We are happy that humans are becoming more aware, more sensitive, more gentle.

Swim with us in your mind hearts.

We are always there. The seal line connection. "Sea" "L" stands for Love. That is our essence – to touch one another in gentleness and love. You saw that yesterday – a glimpse in the day of the Pacific seal.

We sea lions are also here as ambassadors of the sea. Come be with us in the love of the ocean seas.

Seals, Sea Lions: Goodbye, we are always here.

Also from Margaret:

I DRAW BIG SYMBOLS in the hard sand at Pacifica Beach. It is easy to draw them. A joy!

There is only one interruption. An older man walks by and asks what are these symbols for and I tell him they are gifts to the ocean from the Native Americans. He says the symbols should be put on a billboard at the entrance to the beach.

As I draw the symbols on the sand, I speak to the ocean about what I am doing. When I finish, I end with the whale symbol, the Universal Law of Movement and Balance. The ocean responds with large powerful waves. All the surfers are happy. The feeling is joyfulness.

A hawk cries two times -- or is it an eagle?

It is hard to leave Pacifica Beach, one of the most powerful beaches of all.

Barbara Journal:

After leaving Pacifica Beach, and driving to San Francisco to reach the Golden Gate Bridge, we see the tops of the bridge, but for some reason we do not reach it. Signs tell us where to go until the signs stop and then we have to continue along with the thought that we will find the bridge somehow. We MUST reach it in order to cross it.

Well, we drive longer than expected and finally we reach the famous Golden Gate Bridge. While we are driving on it, we are surprised to find many pedestrians walking on a bridge sidewalk, following the railing.

On the other side of the bridge, we are surprised to begin driving on steep, mountain-like cliffs. Up and down, up and down, sharp bends and curves. Yes, this is spectacular scenery to view when one dares to look away from the road. We need to reach the house of friends even though they will not be at home. We are disappointed but we must put down a Beacon of Light, the vortexes, as well as play the sacred music. We are finishing our journey's work which has been satisfactory.

A snowstorm delayed us but that obstacle was soon overcome. We came, we put down the vortexes, made the Beacons of Light, played the sacred music, talked with the ocean and the sea creatures. This journey will always remain in our hearts.

Chapter 2

Africa ~ Uganda

<u>Barbara Journal:</u>

February 3:

We have been urged by the Higher Worlds to immediately place an esoteric belt around the African Continent.

Why?

To prevent the Great Rift from splitting.

How are we to do this?

Actually, we realize the technique can be easy. When a woman puts on stockings, what is she doing? Encircling her legs. With our minds, we make a one-leg stocking and fit it around Africa.

We know thought is energy. It exists and because of the Law of Cause and Effect, what exists has to be counted. And so, from top to bottom we have encircled the continent of Africa with a tight stocking. That is what we have done, and we feel comfortable. It keeps the African continent from splitting into two pieces via the Great Rift Valley that contains the Nile River origin as well as the location of the Equator.

We will begin an African journey by flying to Uganda located in East Africa. Visiting the Nile River origin will be part of this journey. First we will fly to Chicago to board a Qatar Air flight directly to Doha in the Middle East. On arrival, we will wait about six hours before boarding another Qatar Air flight taking us directly to Uganda.

By email, we are in close touch with Mike and Ruth Ssembiro of Uganda whom we met in December at a conference in Lucknow, India called Confluence 2013. The Ssembiros have arranged to transport us from the Ugandan airport to Kampala, the capital, where we will stay at the Hotel International.

Also, they will take us to a newly built school in a remote area of the country. We have learned there is excitement about us coming to see the new school. A few weeks ago, when emailing Mike, we suggested that the community help with the physical building of the school. Parents who help should register their children to attend. Our suggestion has born fruit.

We want to take gifts to the children, and so we have gone to Staples, an office supply company, to buy lightweight gifts to transport in our suitcases -- many pencils, some pencil sharpeners, and some pens. Staples wants us to take paper for the children, but we know the weight would be too heavy for our bags. Later, in Uganda, maybe we can find a place with paper. In any case, February 4 we will begin our journey to Uganda. While there, we will talk to Mike and Ruth about the importance of having a peace pole planted and a flag ceremony. This broadcasts peace to the world which at this moment needs this type of broadcasting. Maybe the President of the country will accept an invitation to attend a ceremony.

February 4:

Today begins our journey, and, we are not leaving at the usual time of 6 or 7 a.m. Hurray! We are leaving at 5:10 p.m. Luxury!

Taxi driver Mr. Dependable picks us up and drives us to the airport where we are quickly through Security, etc., and waiting at the gate for our flight. Will it be late? Because recent weather has been awful for air traffic, many flights are late or even cancelled at the last minute. Well, our flight arrives and that's all that matters.

We fly to Chicago's O'Hare Airport without difficulty and then we board a Qatar Airways flight to Doha, Qatar. From there we take a direct flight to Uganda. We know our Chicago to Doha flight will be a long one ending after midnight.

On arrival at Doha, we are astonished at the size of this airport. Personnel are ready to assist us and we know that without them, we could not have reached the proper terminal and gate for our flight to Uganda. It is interesting to us that workmen are busily expanding this huge airport. It is the middle of the night and they are working as diligently as if it is daytime.

We climb aboard our Qatar Airways flight and we seat ourselves to begin a flight to Entebbe Airport located on the map at the 'bottom' of Uganda. This airport is separated from Kampala, the capital. Why are the two separated? There must be a legitimate reason but we don't understand it.

When we reach Uganda, I am awake looking out the window at darkness. I feel there are trees down there although I cannot see them. I think we will not be landing in a desert. When the pilot, who has been flying high, begins lowering us for a landing, I see lights here and there on the dark ground. People are living down there.

The darkness has lifted when we do arrive at Entebbe. I see few planes parked at the airport. As for ground personnel, I see none. Maybe it is too early for workers to be at their jobs.

In any case, we are soon off the plane and filing into the terminal where there are officials who give Margaret and me visas, and others who pass us quickly through Security. We follow signs telling us where to exit the terminal, and at the doorway Ruth and Mike Ssembiro are waiting to drive us to our hotel at Kampala. Wonderful to see them! We had such a good time with them in India last December and we know we will have a good time with them in their homeland of Uganda.

We load our bags and ourselves into their car and we are quickly on our way to Kampala -- on the wrong side of the road, as I would call driving the British way. Uganda, after all, was a possession of the British Empire, and so one would assume that driving in Uganda would be according to the British system.

Few are driving on the roads today, and we make good headway until we come close to Kampala where the traffic becomes heavier and heavier. I note the number of motorcycles on the road, and I soon realize that many, a great many, are used as quick, cheap taxis. It seems that a potential customer negotiates a price with the driver and then jumps aboard behind the driver so that soon the motorcycle is roaring along, weaving this way and that way through the car traffic until the destination is reached. Then the rider gets off the motorcycle and the driver starts looking for another customer.

Another way to reach a destination without a car is to take a white van that acts as a taxi for multiple customers traveling at the same time. Maybe ten customers. The van stops at certain specific places along the road to pick up customers, and probably the van stops at destinations requested by the customers.

When we reach the outskirts of Kampala, Mike, who is driving us, turns sharply and stops at a closed gate which is quickly opened for us. We are at the Hotel International where Margaret and I will stay for the next five days.

Interesting, at the hotel doorway for us to walk through to reach the lobby, there is a Security scanner, the type one finds at airports. Of course the device gives a warning signal when scanning us, as one can expect, because we have in our pockets coins and other 'suspicious' items. A quick check by a woman in charge wearing an official uniform is enough for her to allow us to enter. And, by the way, over the next few days, when we encounter her security scanner and it gives a warning signal, she allows us to enter anyway without a security swipe from her. We know she is using her intuition that tells her we are okay to pass. We find intuition to be heavily used in Uganda.

Friendly front desk personnel give us a room on the 'first floor', which means we walk downstairs to our room rather than upstairs. Our room faces a swimming pool just below us, and here, near the swimming pool in the early evening, we have dinner with Ruth and Mike. Then, to bed. TIRED.

We started our journey on February 4 and now it is the evening of February 6. Yes. We are TIRED.

February 7:

Our room has two comfortable beds with mosquito netting over both. We do not hear or see any insects. GOOD. Years ago, when I was living in Africa, I contacted malaria. One time having that disease is enough for a lifetime. I want good mosquito netting at this Hotel International and we have it!

It is time for breakfast, and we eat in a large hotel dining area overlooking lofty trees growing close to the windows. Big, perched birds look in at us and we look out at them.

After breakfast Mike returns and we are excitedly giving him an idea that has occurred to us. In June, he is in charge of a big art competition at the Uganda Museum. We think a peace pole should be planted there in June. We think the President of Uganda should be invited to the art competition and the planting of the peace pole.

We emphasize that there is good reason to have competition among the children followed by a peace pole planting. They will compete in a positive manner and then all will plant a peace pole together. When they are adults, this experience may help them solve conflicts in a positive manner rather than invoking violence so prevalent on the planet today. Mike likes this idea, and so we compose a letter to be given to the President. Then he drives us close to the President's office to deliver the letter while we wait in the car watching Ugandans walking back and forth on the sidewalk beside our parked car. It is fun doing this. We note how well they treat each other. We see smiles.

When Mike returns, he tells us the President is with others at a retreat for one week in order to decide how the government will be run in 2014. Mike also tells us we need to include our biographies with the letter because the President and his associates have no idea who we are. And so Mike takes us to a busy Internet cafe where computers are handy for people to use, and we use one of them to write our bios.

It is now 2:30 p.m., and we are hungry! Margaret has spotted a nearby Turkish restaurant that looks new, and here we treat Mike to an excellent Turkish meal. The owner and another male, both Turks, come to speak with us as we are eating. What fun!

Afterward, we do not return to the President's office because we realize that Mike needs to include his biography with ours. Well, that can be done later. Now he drives us to the Uganda Museum where the art competition for children will take place in June. The museum is in Kampala itself but not in an area of high-rise buildings. When we arrive, Margaret and I immediately realize the extensive grass grounds of the museum would be a good place to plant a peace pole.

Inside the museum, a surprise awaits us. In one of the glass cases is Lucy, estimated to have lived 3.2 million years ago. Is this the real Lucy, or is it a replica? For us, we prefer that this skeleton is the real Lucy, and so we do not ask.

Upstairs, we meet the directress in charge of the museum, and we tell her about our desire to have a peace pole planted here in June during the children's art competition. We realize she likes this idea, and we understand when she diplomatically says that if the 'top brass' accept the idea, then she will accept it, too. We know it will take time to 'sort things out' between various government officials, and we will wait patiently for a decision about planting the peace pole.

February 8:

We have breakfast this morning looking out the windows at lofty trees with big, perched birds looking in at us. Today we will go to a sparsely populated area to visit the Kasangula Talent School built in two weeks by the community. A teacher has come to teach the children, and the school has been in session one week. Mike and Ruth pick us up, and before we head for the school, we return to the government buildings in Kampala where Ruth, Margaret and I sit at an outdoor cafe waiting for a friend of the President to meet us. He arrives and now we discover an amazing fact. He speaks British English from the 'old days', and we speak American English. He does not understand our dialect and we do not understand his. Fortunately, Ruth is with us and can interpret. But, how amazing that this English incompatibility has happened! Then, the private secretary of the Vice President arrives, and he cannot understand us any better than we can understand him! Ruth again saves the day.

After this brief encounter with little said between us because we speak different dialects, we are on our way to Kasangula. It is not close and at first the traffic is heavy, but eventually there is less traffic. When we reach a dirt road, there is no traffic. Mike puts a handkerchief over his face to ward off the dust, and we know he will be happy when rain comes to settle the dust that is so prevalent in Uganda. He tells us they are encountering a drought because there has been little rain lately.

When we reach the new school, Margaret and I would have passed it without giving it a glance. It is set back from the road about fifty feet and is made of papyrus with a tin roof. However, Mike knows we are at the location of the small school and there are children and parents waiting for us. We estimate that the school children are between four and nine years old. How exciting to be here!

The children are happy and they race to meet us and begin leading us to the school. We meet Mike's brother who is the new teacher. He has quit his teaching job to come here to teach the children. Two small girls hand us a beautiful bouquet of flowers.

Inside the school the children individually introduce themselves by name in English! They have learned how to do this and they have only attended school one week. Margaret and I hand our gift of pencils to each student, and some pencil sharpeners and pens. We also have for them thirty colored photographs taken from calendars. Usually, I save calendar photographs for the children of India, but today they go to Ugandan children for the walls of their new school. We give scotch tape to the teacher so the photographs will go on the walls. He asks us to sign the guest book. We also shake hands with each student. Snap, snap go cameras. The moment of being here at this remarkable place in the middle of nowhere will remain with us forever.

Now we all walk outside the tiny school to join the parents of the children and we watch the children begin a little performance of singing two songs in English. Yes, this afternoon of joy in this Ugandan undeveloped area is something to remember always. We are tired when we return to our hotel and we go to bed early. Even though we cannot remember our dreams, we know they are sweet dreams.

February 9:

Today is Sunday and we will visit a church to hear Gospel music. I must admit I am unprepared for this experience, which is awesome.

The church service has already begun when we arrive, and this service is so heavily attended, there is hardly room available for us on the long benches that spread across the inside of the building. We squeeze into spaces in the back.

This is my first attendance of Gospel music in a church. The ENTHUSIASM for singing is so intense, tears come to my eyes. As they sing, the hearts of the people are wide open with LOVE. On and on and on, they sing. Some lift their arms and hands as they are singing.

YES. A MEMORABLE MOMENT FOR ME!

After church, we eat a quick lunch at Mike and Ruth's house before Mike begins driving us to the source of the Nile River. I am excited to visit this place. Traffic on Kampala roads is, as usual, heavy, but not unbearable this Sunday afternoon, and we go along smartly for over an hour. Then we stop at a town gas station because something is wrong with the car. Mike knows this town, and especially he knows a mechanic. We wait while he summons the mechanic, and then we sit on a bench near the gas pumps while the mechanic examines the car and quickly finds the problem. There is a disconnection of wires. Required items for fixing the problem are available in town, and in less than a half hour, these items have been retrieved. But, the problem persists.

We remain sitting on the gas station bench watching matters unfold, and especially watching a big, fully-grown, heavy, white, fluffy hen race across the busy highway, skirting traffic to come to weeds near us that will provide food. We cluck at her and she is not afraid. She does not want us to pet her, but she is not afraid.

On another long bench facing the gas pumps are seated four males who obviously know each other well. Their backs rest against the gas station building as they talk with each other. After a time, the hen goes near them and we no longer can see her. Will the men scare her? Will they think of eating her? Finally, I can no longer resist getting up to see what has happened to the hen. I walk to the men and ask where is she and they point to her fast asleep at their feet. I am surprised, and I tell the men that I am worried about the hen. They smile and tell me she is their friend. Meaning, they are used to their friend the hen sleeping near them. The oldest of the four men stands and goes to Mike and Ruth's car being repaired. After a time, he returns to tell us that everything is all right and the car will be ready soon. This little event at the gas station has given Margaret and me a look into the patience of Ugandans and their persistence. We are seeing people who do not give up. When the car is ready to leave, we climb into the back seat and we are soon on our way to the source of the Nile.

The afternoon has moved along until we are beginning to realize that the end of daylight will soon be with us. And yes, we arrive at the source of the Nile exactly as the bright red sun is ready to go below the horizon. A boatman puts us in his boat and we are quickly at the exact source where water is coming out of Mother Earth and whirling around so that some water goes north and some water goes south. This is the source of the Nile. An exciting experience!

Within thirty feet of the source of the Nile is a tiny island with bushy trees that depend on the Nile's water. These trees look very healthy. Because it is time for the day to end, big birds are already in place on the branches of these trees to rest for the night. Many are big white, fluffy birds. I do not know their species.

Tardy birds begin rushing to the trees to take a place for the night with their bird friends. There is no sound of objection even though the branches of the trees are already heavily covered by birds and so the late comers must squash themselves onto the branches.

February 10:

Today Mike takes us to the Greenhill Academy located within the Kampala area. When we arrive, we park at a big lot for cars but only two cars are parked. Why would an academy have such a big parking area when there are no cars? Later, when we leave the academy, the parking lot is full of cars. Who owns these cars, we ask? The parents of the Greenhill Academy students who have come to pick up their children when school ends for the day. How different this is from the situation at the Kasagula Talent School where parents have no cars.

We enter the school and meet teachers and students. At one classroom, a large, blank, white paper is produced and students are asked to make a mural. Without hesitation, they begin drawing one. Obviously, this is not the first time they have drawn a mural.

The teacher shows us a large, unopened package that has just arrived from Japan. Ugandan and Japanese students are cooperating by painting a mural.

Good!

Before we leave the school, we meet and speak with the head mistress of the academy. She likes the idea of planting a peace pole at her academy.

February 11:

Mike drives us to the Entebbe Airport for us to board our Qatar Airlines flight to Doha. We will miss Mike and Ruth.

After we arrive home and turn on our computers, we learn that Ruth has sent us an email.

Dear Margaret and Barbara,

Greetings and love to you from Uganda. Hope you are all well. We are all fine here. It started raining this week, the dust is reducing and the weather is calm. Birds are singing in the air! We hope to plant some food at Kasangula for our home consumption and for the school, too. The children come with cold food which they pack for their lunch with the porridge that we provide at school. The cold food is not healthy for their health. We therefore want to plant enough food so that we can be able to provide both food and porridge to our children. We believe this will also boost their learning. There is a lot to do there as you also saw, but we shall prioritize all the activities and handle one by one. Ruth

CHAPTER 3

AFRICA ~ UGANDA

M̲a̲r̲g̲a̲r̲e̲t̲ ̲J̲o̲u̲r̲n̲a̲l̲:

February 1:

I am in transition between California and the Pacific Ocean and Uganda, a land-locked country with the headwaters of the Nile and location of Lake Victoria.

I ask the whales to comment:

Their answer: *This is a time of change and a time of movement and balance. Whales are the Guardians of the Universal Symbol of Movement and Balance. That is why we are here at every crossroad. We can be your Guidance System in the long trip you undertake. Think of our long trips and then you will lessen your thought of length and shortness of time. On our travels we release the codings for humanity – for the life forms on Mother Earth. Our codings are more refined, complex, intricate at every turn. A library in each whale, a guidance system for the future. Whales are needed for the balance of Mother Earth. We are the gyroscope bringing Nature in a balanced plane. The heart sets the course, the mind can help or hinder. Guard the mind. Do not let fear, pre-planning anxiety slip in.*

Whale presence can be felt in Uganda. It is a matter of frequency. The people are very heart-centered and can easily pick up Love frequencies of the Sea and Land Creatures.

Look at the Sea Lions, how every moment they expressed love to one another. Yes, the males can be aggressive, territorial, but only when this is called for. Their resting state is peace and balance in their being-ness.

Humans in their resting state may not be restful. In the mindset, is the dial set to worry, overwhelmed-ness, fear? Look to the whales, dolphins, seals, sea lions, and otters for guidance. Earth has been given the gift of their presence, the master teachers of love and wellbeing. They move, they stay in one place, they live well if they are not blocked or interfered with.

Honor your teachers of the oceans. Rest in their love. Give them love and greetings. That is why you saw your teachers -- the loving pair of sea lions nuzzling check to check below on the wharf of Santa Cruz. And when you saw the blind dancing seal in the Moody Pyramids Aquarium who danced her heart song as a gift to the Mother Earth and to the people who understood. Bless these beings. They are your way-showers to the Higher Dimensions.

Blessings for the day from the Whales Universal.

February 4:

The trip begins. The weather in Rochester is cold and bright. We are told a big snowstorm is coming and so we drive very early to the airport to get our boarding passes.

When it is time to fly, Mr. Dependable returns to the airport and we board.

The pilot says there will be strong headwinds, which will probably extend our flight to Chicago. Snow, he says, has come to Chicago from the West -- a big snowstorm.

On the plane, I sing to the wind – soft, beautiful songs, 'The Ash Grove' and 'Swing Lo, Sweet Chariot', and I ask the wind for a smooth passage so we can catch our plane for overseas. I learn that 90% of the flights are coming into Chicago and 40% of the planes are leaving. I feel the big international flights will go. When we reach Chicago we circle a long time before landing in the snow. It is still snowing. The runways are snow-covered but there are no blizzard conditions. When we do land and change to a Qatar flight, this plane has two sessions of de-icing before leaving. Barbara says it is 12:00 midnight. We feel blessed to be on our way. I think the winds, the whales, the dolphins, the Higher Worlds tempered the storm.

When we land at Doha to transfer to another Qatar Airways flight to reach Uganda, it is after midnight.

February 6, 6:30 a.m.:

We arrive in Uganda at Entebbe Airport and Ruth and Mike Ssembiro meet us to drive us to the capital Kampala where we will stay at Hotel International 2000, LTD. Because of heavy traffic, the drive is long and we have a chance to see a slice of Ugandan life.

When I finally reach our hotel room, I want to put down the complete set of Vortexes for the country, among them the symbols of Spiritual Strength, Health and Happiness, Spiritual Protection of the Family, etc.

After the symbols have been put down, I need to put my mind on the crack, the Great Riff. I want channeling and now I ask, Can we speak about the crack?

Answer from the Higher Worlds: *Yes. It is necessary to hold the continent intact.*

Question: Do the people understand the crack?

Answer: *They will comprehend it in time, as will the New Yorkers understand the rise in sea level. Mother Earth's forces move slowly or quickly. It depends on the emotions of the inhabitants in the area. Fear should not be introduced for that only exacerbates the problem. Africans are very intuitive so they will pick up the concern of the crack.*

Lake Victoria from space is the entry point of positive energy of love healing Light for Africa. It must be surrounded with positive energy because it is the Shield of Africa.

Every time one sees the map of Africa, one can envision this powerful energy spreading across the land, above and below and through all boundaries, dissolving all boundaries of people, country, religious identities. One continent, a harmony of peace, prosperity, cooperation through friendship.

The heart shield of Africa, Lake Victoria, pinpoints the access and distribution of Love.

The Vortexes help to enhance this power. They transmit harmony and Peace, Love and Light.

Lake Victoria serves the continent in richness of health and vitality. It is the headwaters of the Nile. Through this service of the Nile, Peace, Love and Light flow to the Mediterranean through the conduit of the ageless water that flows through history.

The channeling switches to remarks about the sun:

The sunrise brings the neutrinos that are changed to Love Energy and can be done by the humans here and also by the Higher Worlds Brothers and Sisters in a cooperative manner.

Remember the Sun Disc of Mount Kilimanjaro and the power source of Light, the tempering modulation, enhancer of Peace and Wellbeing.

While I am receiving this channeling, in my hand, I have Vortexes sending out the energies – Universal Law of Light, Sound and Vibration, Universal Law of Free Will, Spiritual Freedom of Man, Universal Law of Symmetry, Spiritual Law of Equality, and the Vortex of Right Relationship.

Now, Emma Kunz channels information to me on ascension to the higher dimensions. She says, *Remember Labyrinth, the children's game where one turns the surface board to move around obstacles of prejudice, hated, separation. When one goes to judgment, one drops in the holes of the third dimension. One must stay on the light, love, peace frequency to reach the fifth dimension and link to the Brothers and Sisters.*

7:30 p.m., we have dinner with Mike and Ruth by the swimming pool at our hotel. Afterward, because Barbara and I are so tired, we climb into our comfortable beds with full mosquito netting over them. The fan is on to cool us. We are happy to be here.

February 7:

We have early breakfast in the main dining room with an amazing view of the sunrise. There are big trees with many big birds. I eat spaghetti, beans, peanut butter, toast, black tea and mango juice. As I am eating, the sky turns to soft pink and blue and gold -- pre-dawn colors announcing a fireball sunrise over Lake Victoria.

After breakfast, Mike comes and we write a letter to the President about a peace pole planting and flag ceremony. Mike plans to deliver it to the President's office. However, when he delivers it, he learns that we need a letter of introduction with our bios.

He drives us to an Internet café where we can use a computer to write a letter to the President. We also make a copy of the cover of one of our earlier books because it shows our photographs. During all of this, I see a dragonfly signifying transformation and a butterfly signifying change. We need this. We want the President to agree to a peace pole and flag ceremony.

We have lunch at a nearby Turkish restaurant and here we tell Mike that he should be a panelist for the November 1 Gathering of the

World Brotherhood Union in Istanbul. Barbara is an advisor for the four panelists.

As a PS to this, Barbara does recommend Mike and he has been chosen to be one of the four panelists.

After lunch Mike drives us the Uganda Museum so we can check where to plant a peace pole and have a flag ceremony in June. We meet the museum supervisor who says she will approve a peace pole and flag ceremony if higher government officials agree. At the museum, we briefly see Lucy, an ancient skeleton and we also enjoy pictures of ancient cave art reminding me of Australian Aboriginal art. A woman begins playing beautiful music by using a wooden xylophone and a one-string fiddle. We enjoy this tremendously.

February 8:

This morning Mike and Ruth drive us to an outdoor café to meet government officials to talk about a peace pole planting and flag ceremony at the museum. While we are there, great birds are circling overhead -- hawks, vultures, storks, etc. I see a huge beetle at my feet.

Later, when I am typing my notes of the journey, I have an amazing understanding. In ancient Egyptian times, the beetle is the patron of the sun, creation, life and resurrection. I realize now the beetle can hold the Vortexes as he did the Sun in ancient times. In my mind, the beetle has come back again for 2014 – eternal and present. Now I address the beetle in my mind: Thank you, Beetle, for coming out that day in Uganda.

The Beetle answers: *You are welcome. Thank you for 'seeing' me.*

The Golden Brown Beetle.

Hmmmmmm. I think there is no time and space. Everything is present.

In the afternoon, we drive into the countryside where there is a new school, the Kasangula Talent School. A banner is at the entrance and Ruth takes a photograph.

Before entering the small school, we meet parents of the students. We also meet Mike's brother, who is warm and friendly. Two little girls give us a bouquet of flowers and greet us in English saying, "We welcome you. We hope you are happy. Welcome to our new school!"

Mike's brother takes us into the school built in two weeks with a tin roof and papyrus reed walls. There are two tiny classrooms with chalkboard space and a table and benches. All the children introduce themselves with their names and class. We give out the pencils, sharpeners, pens and bright animal calendar pictures to the delight of everyone. The teacher will hang the pictures on the wall.

We are asked to sign the guest book and we are the school's first guests. I write in the guestbook, "A miracle", and draw a heart. To me, it is a miracle this school has been built in two weeks.

Outside the school, we sit in a circle of chairs and benches under trees to listen to two drums and the children singing welcoming songs in English. I have tears with the joy of it.

We have a long drive back to the hotel and go to bed early. A Blessed Day!

Midnight, Emma channels: *Keep an eye on the prize. The education of the children lifts the entire country up and out of poverty and degradation of the environment.*

February 9:

This morning Mike, Ruth and their son Andrew take us to a Pentecostal Church near Lake Victoria. It is Sunday. As we arrive, great gospel singing is pouring out the doors. The place is stuffed with people singing love and admiration. As we enter the church, Barbara gives to a door greeter our bouquet of flowers from the

Kasangula school children. We sit on benches at the back of this very full church. During the service, I take the power of the music and the love of the congregation and place this on Lake Victoria to send it up the Nile River to all the countries of Africa and the Middle East. When the service is over and we leave the church, we are greeted by many people happy to meet us.

We return to Mike and Ruth's home to have a brief lunch before beginning our drive to the headwaters of the Nile. It is a long, arduous trip, and before we arrive, the car breaks down in a town near a gas station. The starter is broken. Mike calls a mechanic friend who comes immediately with his assistant. Barbara and I sit on a bench at the gas station to watch the repair work that takes two plus hours.

When finally we are ready to leave, it is nearly sunset. We drive through dense forest and lush country to finally arrive at the source of the Nile. Here we see the deep currents where underground springs feed the Nile. We cannot see Lake Victoria but we know the lake is in the far distance.

I quietly read the Vortexes at the bank of the river, addressing both the Nile and Lake Victoria, and saying these Vortexes are gifts for the Nile, Uganda, the Middle East, and all of Africa.

The golden sun is setting as we board a small boat taking us to the exact source of the Nile. On small islands here I see many birds -- great egrets, white and black cormorants, herons, cranes and ibis. The trees are packed with them. It is the end of the day and all will be together on the branches of the trees at the source of the Nile.

We are here with the Nile River flowing out of Uganda up to Egypt. Past to present to future. The Nile and ancient Egypt continue on. I sing Master Goi's song, May Peace Prevail On Earth.

February 10:

Today we drive to the Greenhill Academy in Kampala to meet a teacher and children we met two months ago in Lucknow, India. In their classroom they show us excellent artwork and crafts. Photographs are taken of the teacher and Barbara and me holding a large painting of a silhouette of the African continent with trees and a sky of green and red. In the center is an image of a white bird, an ibis.

It is a joyous visit to Greenhill Academy. Earlier in India, the teacher had invited us to the source of the Nile but he could not come with us. We are happy to be with him in his classroom today.

Later, after we have left the Greenhill Academy, Emma speaks to me.

You have built a powerful force field. You have lit the pilot light for the Victoria Nile Africa stove. Pilot Light of Joy, Truth, Harmony. Rejoice in mission accomplished.

The Angels of the Nile know. The Guardian of Victoria Lake knows. The birds rejoice. They have been recognized for their splendor. They showed their babies to you, their nests. A butterfly flew in the art class.

Sleep. The next journey begins. I am with you. Rejoice in the trip.

February 11:

Mike picks us up at the hotel to drive us to the airport. There is no traffic and we move along smoothly.

At the airport, we say goodbye to Mike who has taken us everywhere. While climbing the stairs to reach departure gates, I see a tree full of weaverbirds with their hanging round nests. I stop to see them. Such a fantastic sight!

CHAPTER 4

THE MIDDLE EAST QATAR

Barbara Journal:

February 11:

Today we will begin a short visit to Qatar in the Middle East. I do not know this predominately Muslim country and I am happy to visit. Years ago I lived in North Africa and for a short time in Lebanon. The latter was when there was strife between the Syrians and Egyptians. I remember seeing people fleeing Syria in cars whose roofs were piled with possessions. I remember one car with only a wooden chair attached to the top. Was this the only material possession deemed worth saving?

When I lived in North Africa, there was no strife, no fighting. Everyone was pleasant with everyone. I was a woman not veiled and no one minded. Well, things have changed. People are fighting each other. Muslims are fighting each other. My country is fighting. Qatar, I understand, has no violence within its borders. I want to put my foot on the Middle East to see how it 'feels' now.

We can be in Qatar the middle of February, on Valentine's Day, a day of love. We can spread the energy of love throughout the region to help reduce tension.

Just now, we are in Uganda and Mike drives us to Entebbe Airport for our 1:05 p.m. flight to Doha, capital of Qatar. For our flight, we arrive early at the airport and we have a chance to sit and watch passengers come and go. Outside a window we see a very big, grey U.S. military plane land and roll past us. Everyone is watching and no one makes remarks. Why has this plane landed here? It looks like it is carrying a lot of passengers. Soldiers, no doubt. Why have they arrived here in Uganda? Then I am thinking that maybe if they are stationed in neighboring Rwanda or some other neighboring country, there are no airfields where they can safely land, and so they must land in Uganda and drive overland to their destination. In any case, we sit and watch activity at the Entebbe Airport and then we board and take our assigned seats to ride to Doha where we will stay six days.

It is a cloudless day and we sit comfortably as the pilot flies us North. When we reach the Persian Gulf, we know we will be landing soon. Iran is clearly spread out below us, and we look out the window at this place that would be interesting to visit, but our country and Iran are hardly on speaking terms, which cuts the chances of visiting.

6:15 p.m. the pilot lands us at the Doha, Qatar airport, and from the cockpit, he announces that we have arrived on time. We file out of our plane and take our places at Security to have our passports checked and to buy visas. The line we join is VERY LONG. At least three hundred passengers. Were they all from our plane? I think not. There seems to be many planes landing at this airport.

We note that those in line with us are mostly males. I estimate eighty percent are males. Who are they, and why aren't they traveling with their wives? Well, we are in the Middle East and wives are less seen here than in other places in the world.

Also of interest, to my knowledge it is not the custom of Muslim men to look at women. Well, Margaret and I are in line with many males, and we are not wearing headscarves to hide our faces. Are the males making a point of looking at us? No. It is not their custom.

When it is time for us to reach the head of the long line, we are issued visas via credit card payment. Our passports are stamped and we go through Security to enter the busy part of the terminal. We have reservations to stay at the Ramada Encore Hotel in Doha, and we phone the hotel asking about a shuttle between the airport and the hotel. Yes, there will be a shuttle and it will arrive soon. We are told to stand at a certain place outside the terminal. Okay, fine, we understand, but, just now we are spotting a money change booth, a welcome sight, and we head toward the booth to change dollars into Qatar money.

We walk no more than twenty feet and a man approaches asking if we are Barbara Wolf. YES! Who is this man? He explains that he is the shuttle driver and he has been on his cell phone with the hotel when we phoned. Amazing!

We change money and then we follow him to his shuttle. Along the way, we learn he is from the Philippines. I know that over the years many looking for work have headed to Qatar because there is always much work available here.

As we ride along, we are looking out the windows at this city that has sprung up from nearly nothing not too long ago. We see skyscrapers and other modern city facilities, and we see many cars. Few people are walking. I know the climate is mild here and I am thinking the temperature is a bit below normal. However, a light coat is all that is needed.

At the hotel, the Front Desk gives us Room 210 on the second floor, and we are soon reaching it by elevator. We are following a hotel clerk who has our bags and the key to our room which he opens. We see a relatively small room and we feel something unexpected -- cold. The room is cold. How can it be so cold in this hot country? We ask for the air conditioning to be turned off and we are told it is turned off. We ask for heating to be put on and we are told there are no heaters. Oh dear! Well, we can survive.

We are tired. Today has been a long one. We need rest. The two beds in this room will soon be occupied.

February 12:

This morning we direct our attention to a large dining area to eat a buffet breakfast, and I must say, the food here is superb! There are at least thirty selections. I take a bit of salmon, a boiled egg, fruit of various types, etc. Mint tea to drink. The waiter, who is from Sri Lanka, shows me he has put fresh mint in my teapot of hot water. Delicious!

After breakfast, we put our attention on visiting the Museum of Islamic Art, and we hire a taxi driver parked outside the hotel to take us to this majestic, huge building four storeys high. My primary desire is to see Islamic calligraphy, and I am not disappointed! NEVER have I seen such work! It is displayed here with careful deliberation, and slowly one walks on and on and on enjoying this fantastic sight. Later, when I visit the bookstore, I find a beautiful book of calligraphy compiled by Mohamed Zakariya, a Muslim American who exhibited in this museum in 2012.

Margaret and I are slow to leave this museum. When our feet are tired of walking, we sit for a time beside a great window looking out at water. Is this a newly constructed arm of the Persian Gulf? Imagination is high in Doha. One can expect almost anything.

Our taxi man is on schedule to return us to the hotel where we take an elevator to the eleventh floor to sit next to a large indoor swimming pool. No one except us is up here to swim or to relax on available reclining chairs. We sit and put our faces to the sunshine which our room cannot give us. The only window in our room looks out at an airshaft.

Are there available rooms to get sunshine? Maybe, but we do not ask. We think our room gives us what is given to most Muslim women -- involuntary solitary confinement. We want to taste how they live.

I remember remarks stemming from Brazil when I first visited that country years ago. With little on to attract eligible males for marriage, young women promenade the beaches. Once married, that is the end of promenading. They are shut in. I note today that Brazilian women drive and walk the streets and behave in the same manner as women in most areas of the world. Maybe someday Muslim women will no longer have to live in involuntary solitary confinement once they are married.

February 13:

For us, today is camel market day, and we are excited to see the camels. Our taxi driver, the same one as yesterday, tells us there are 5,000 camels. Well, I think that is an exaggeration, but when we do reach the market, there are MANY. Tall males with great, extending necks, female camels, baby camels. SO MANY! Why are there so many? Even a need to make a camel caravan does not take so many camels. Of course Qatar sits next to the huge desert of Saudi Arabia, but even a huge desert does not require so many camels. To be sold here, where did all these camels come from?

Horses are another matter. We see few, but we see hundreds of wool sheep standing, not moving, fenced in like one great lump. We see no food for them. None are eating. I conclude they are collected here to be sold and slaughtered for their wool and for eating.

Well, the camels are eating. There is plenty of food for them. I leave the market with mixed feelings. It is wonderful seeing camels, but the sheep? No.

When we leave the market, our taxi driver points out buildings here and there, and we briefly visit the Katara area, location of a cultural village that promotes world cultures to help bring peace and global understanding.

Now it is time to visit one of the largest mosques in Doha. When we reach it, few are there, probably because it is not the holy day of Friday, but early Thursday morning. Our taxi driver says people will begin gathering here on the great outer courtyard around 11:30 a.m. in order to enter the mosque interior for a service. He tells us 10,000 could gather here. Wow!

The taxi driver continues driving us through the city pointing out buildings here and there. Pointing out the extensive, on-going construction of new buildings. I think of the government office in charge of making new maps for the city. That office must be frustrated with all the new buildings!

February 14, Valentine's Day:

Today is the day we have been waiting for, a day of Love.

At 11:30 a.m., we are upstairs on the eleventh floor with the swimming pool behind us as we look out at the blue sky and the sunshine. We begin playing the sacred music called Musical Rapture. Fifteen minutes into the music, the Angel Kingdom singers come in. We have reached the point of anti-matter. When this anti-matter is combined with the energy of third dimensional matter, Zero Point is reached. Now is the moment to use this combination to present the positive energies of Love to the Middle East.

As the music continues and my mind is on sending out the positive energy of love, a miracle happens.

I am hearing the singing of thousands. I am thinking of the 10,000 visiting the courtyard of the big mosque. Today, Friday, is the holy day for them. When I remove my earphones, I cannot hear the singing. When I put on my earphones, I can hear the singing and the Musical Rapture music. Miracle.

Later, I tell Margaret and she says the same. She has heard the singing, taken off her earphones and not heard the singing, put on her earphones and heard the singing. Miracle.

Our job is to spread the positive energy of Love throughout the Middle East. We have done this.

In the afternoon, our taxi driver takes us again to the Museum of Islamic Art, and as we are riding along, we note that many people are walking, more than earlier. We realize that today is a not a workday in this Muslim country. When we reach the museum, we note that many are here, some with children. And yes, we see husbands and wives walking with each other.

February 15:

Today our taxi driver takes us to the souks, a maze of shops, and even though this is not a day off for work, the souks are active with people. We stop first at shops selling clothes, but this does not interest us. We want to see the birds, especially the falcons. And so our driver, who now has become our walking guide, steers us away from the clothes shops and we are soon in a great cluster of birds and small animals being sold.

We stop at a perch of birds to give them seeds they cannot reach, and they carefully take the seeds from our palms. None try to bite, and certainly none shy away from the food. Then we stop at a cluster of parrots in a big cage, all busily talking at once. When we add our particular birdcall to them, they stop talking to listen.

A cluster of baby rabbits are gathered nearby, and we stop to pet them. I have never seen such tiny rabbits. Have they all just been born? It hardly seems possible, but how can so many little ones be here at the same time?

Our walking guide now takes us to a section of the souks reserved for falcons, and we enter this quiet section and are awed. Blind-folded falcons are shackled to low perches in a large sandbox area. Two falconers are attending to them as well as greeting any potential falcon buyers.

We love this place, and we spend time here watching a potential buyer when he sees a bird of interest to him. He squats down to examine the falcon closely and to give the bird a gentle stroke or two. When we do leave the falcons, we meet a man wearing a traditional Arab, ankle-length robe and headdress who asks if we are falconers and we say no but we love falcons. He tells us he is a member of a falcon group in the U.S.A. and he has recently visited a gathering in Colorado.

Now, our walking guide takes us to nearby stalls of interest to us because it is a resting place for horses. We know this part of the world is famous for its breeding of horses for racing, and for racing itself. We stop to do some petting and the horses do not shy away. They like us. One horse, a black female with white markings, has a strand of hair over one eye, and I think she cannot easily remove it. But we can remove it, and we do. The horse is grateful and her eyes become soft as she looks at us.

In the next stall is a white male with thick curly hair on its back, which is amazing. This hair has been recently combed and it shines, an indication that this horse has been well fed and is in good health.

Yes, visiting the souks today is fun, and we will always remember the falcons and the horses.

CHAPTER 5

THE MIDDLE EAST QATAR

M argaret Journal:

February 11:

We leave Uganda today to take a smooth flight to Doha, Qatar. I am excited to visit this place, especially the new Museum of Islamic Art designed by I.M. Pei. I have watched an interview of this 92-year-old architect giving his concepts for designing the museum. His main focus is on light — sunlight within the framework of a desert environment. He works with geometric forms and latticework that will be a delight to the viewer. He wants the central dome within the museum to be a circle inside a square with a circular lamp framework becoming the central focus below the dome. Tomorrow we expect to visit this museum.

When we reach Doha, we are taken to the Ramada Encore Hotel where we will stay five nights. We are tired! I unpack, take a fast shower and jump into bed under a lot of blankets because it is cold in the room.

February 12:

7:30 a.m., we have a delicious full meal breakfast of omelet, croissants, yogurt, fruit, figs, dates, cheeses, feta, and tea with fresh mint leaves. What a delight! A friendly waiter from Sri Lanka speaks to me about tennis. The professional women's tennis tournament is playing here now in Doha. Are we going? No. His favorite players of earlier times are Pete Sampras and Andre Agassi and I agree with him. We are on the same wavelength.

Midmorning we are taken to the Museum of Islamic Art by a taxi driver who will come for us later. And yes, the new museum is breathtaking. My love of Islamic Art comes roaring back from working in museums in the States. I especially loved the new building at the National Gallery in Washington, D.C. designed by I. M. Pei. Today when we enter the Museum of Islamic Art, we begin viewing calligraphy, decorative textiles, manuscripts, carved screens, ceramic tiles. All are a delight to the eye and of the finest craftsmanship and design.

I think of the artists who produced their artwork, their love of God, their love of their craft and their art. At noontime when we sit quietly in meditation, I use this power of the artists' work to send out peace. I also think of Vortex energy and I combine this with the concept of love, harmony and balance of Islamic Art. I find an amazing blending between this Islamic Art and Vortex concepts.

Afterward, we go to a delightful lunch area in the museum overlooking the water. Here, we speak with a holistic health care doctor from England who is meeting hospital people in Doha to speak to them about healing naturally rather than by over-drugging with standard commercial medicine. When he leaves, we look out the window at the beautiful water spread out below us. Then I look up to the delightful octagonal ceiling window five levels above. Light is pouring in from the central dome that is contained within a square.

In this museum, I am looking at the ceilings, windows, stairs, landings, circular lamp, marble floor tiles, fountains, on and on. Every inch a delight to the mind's eye. I.M. Pei captures the essence of the eternally fresh vibrant beauty of Islamic Art that moves and at the same time rests.

When we return to the hotel, we have a snack and by 3:45 p.m. we are sitting in the bright sunshine pouring into the swimming pool area of the eleventh floor. Here I will give the Vortexes to Qatar and the whole region. I have the Vortex booklet with me.

In meditation, first I call on Emma Kunz to ask how I can unify the energy of the Vortexes with the energies of Muslim cultures in the Middle East:

Her answer: Proceed and let us make the discovery of the unifying principles that can bridge. The link is through the heart. When the mind observes, interferes, it get snared in dates, places and historical events. Let us go beyond the human framework to what is universal. Let us walk this path and see where it leads.

Framework means resonance. The Resonance is Light, Sound and Vibration. To understand resonance, one must have intuition to sense with the heart.

I begin sending out the Vortexes.

Soon Emma interjects: *The mind must be clear to understand the universal underlying principles of Peace, Love and Light. These principles are shared by all mankind.*

Later when I am pondering her comment about sharing Peace, Love and Light, I realize that as humanity changes when achieving a greater understanding between cultures, then a change of heart occurs and humanity grows in compassion and there is Peace.

May Peace Prevail On Earth.

I know geometric form has its basic principles. Light has its basic principles. Love is universal and a wellspring that may be tapped within the hearts of humanity.

May Peace Prevail On Earth.

Creating art is an act of love. Art is a bridge to create peace between peoples.

With my mind, I draw the Vortexes in the water of the swimming pool in front of me on the eleventh floor of the hotel, and I am using my mind to draw the Vortexes in the water of the Gulf and in the world's oceans. I also draw them on the land, in the sand and desert, ancient land. And I also draw them in the air with my mind so that the wind carries the Peace Love vibration to the Middle East to spread Peace, Love and Light.

We are priming the pump of Peace. Qatar is a center for entertainment, sports, and a place for people to gather. Yes, Qatar is a central spot -- world focused.

In the evening we play the Divine Love music to spread the frequencies over the airways to the world.

I receive channeling:

Moving out into the heart space allows everyone to show up. The music penetrates the water, the buildings, the sunset, the sunrise. You will see camels tomorrow. Give music to these heavy workers of the sand.

Continue with your heart wide open. You are with the artisans' love that comes forward to work for the peace in the present time. Time and patience and craftsmanship motivate hope, positive energy, and grace, positive energy. Stay steady. Stay the course. Hold the line steady. Pull in the sail tightly to gain speed.

The frequency of Valentine's Day Love needs to be spread around the world. Love one another as you are loved by us. Love is the energy that makes the flowers grow, the sun to rise, or the planet to turn and receive the sun's light. The birds rejoice in the sun's coming – the flowers, the vegetables turn their heads to the sun. The rhythm of Nature, the strength of Mother Earth, the love of the planet -- a beautiful creation. Be thankful and always present.

Peace be with you.

February 13:

This morning the taxi man drives us to the camel market where we are told there are 5,000 camels for sale. Yes, a lot of camels. Brown, golden, black, white camels, mothers, babies, and teenagers. Gentle sweet camels, but they can be tough. The taxi man stops and pats a tied up camel standing outside a fence. The camel is jumpy and pulls away when we approach. Does he think we will buy him? He does not want that. We keep our distance, honoring the camel's space. A few minutes later we are greeted by a group of young camels who happily come over to the fence to look at us. We see herds of sheep and goats in large pens. The herders are fairly friendly and wave and some smile at us.

Now the taxi driver takes us to the largest mosque in Doha, a beautiful golden structure. We leave the taxi and the taxi driver walks with us. This is his mosque. Now we are greeted by his friend, another young man, a guard who says we must put on a black robe before entering the mosque. We decline this suggestion because we are enjoying the beautiful carving and latticework in the main courtyard. Also, we do not want to stay long because worshipers will come at just before noon and we do not wish to disturb them.

We return to the taxi and our driver continues showing us the city. We see much construction causing dust and debris, and many barriers to the roads because of construction. There seems to be an eternal building of banks, office buildings, sports and shopping complexes, residences, on and on and on.

We drive to the Corniche and see fancy hotel complexes, plus the Qatar ruler's house on its own island or spit of land. This reminds me of the United Arab Emirates with its constructed islands and clustered, elegant residences.

We pass Al Jazeera TV studio and a large soccer stadium. A tennis complex is in the distance. When we reach the Katara Cultural

Village, there is no time to investigate, but the driver gives us an interesting overview of the city.

I do not speak to the driver, but there is a question in my mind. Where are the people? Everyone is in cars. There is traffic. No one is walking on the streets. This is such a contrast from Uganda. Here, there seems to be only one or two motorcycles, whereas in Uganda there are hundreds. When we pass speed roads to Saudi Arabia and Bahrain, our driver comments that people drive 180 to 200 kilometers an hour.

Later in the hotel, we do not want to stay in the room. We feel strange, confined. We have the feeling of women confined to the home looking out behind decorative lattice screens. We do not have decorative lattice screens in our room. The only window looks out at a dark wall.

We return to the eleventh floor to watch the setting sun as we play the Divine Love music. I send love and blessings to the families for balance between males and females so they together can close the day and open another tomorrow.

I receive: *It is not for you to interfere. Just send a mental telegram of love to the people of Qatar and the Middle East. Positive energy. Hope, grace and the feeling of goodness, Love.*

February 14:

Today is Valentine's Day, the day of Love.

Just before noon, we are on the eleventh floor at the swimming pool. Children are playing in the water. We begin listening through our earphones to CDs of the sacred love music. I wait for the Angels on the CD to begin singing. When I hear them, I am ready to send Love and Light energies to the Middle East through my earphones. Then I also hear through my earphones the sound of the Call to Prayer from the Mosque and the singing from the people gathered there. How can this be? It is like a miracle! Later, Barbara tells me she too has heard people singing at the mosque at the same time the Angels are singing. Such a powerful experience! Overwhelming love is pouring out to the Middle East. It is a Gift of Love for Qatar and all the Middle East on Valentine's Day. We will never forget this day.

February 15:

This morning our taxi driver takes us to the Souq Waqif, a large shopping area, to see falcons and Arabian horses. On arrival, we see small parakeets and a dancing parrot that hangs upside down wanting our attention. Then we pass three seated grey parrots whom I call the Three Graces. They look very wise, and they remind me of the Parrots for Peace that sat on the shoulders of firemen fighting the 9/11 fires at the World Trade Center. These parrots I am seeing today want to be with us, want to talk with us. They know we can 'see' them, admire them, and understand them. They do not want us to leave. Nearby, we see Persian kittens, rabbits, puppies, turtles.

Then in a large room we see falcons standing on perches planted on a bed of sand. A white speckled falcon dances on its perch and I have direct contact with it, heart to heart.

In a nearby building, we see two beautiful Arabian horses, one white and the other black with a white blaze. Sohar, the white horse, wants me to touch him. I give him love and affection and tell him he is a beautiful horse. He insists I pet his nose. I am a little shy but he wants it and so I do.

Now we go to another falcon place to watch the care of falcons. A young man tenderly handles them with delicacy and skill.

Our taxi driver does not understand falcons and he begins waving his hands, scaring them so they will flutter. I tell him this is the home of the falcons. All must be kept quiet to keep the falcons quiet and peaceful. I tell him to walk softly, give love, and with his mind, stroke the birds with love and admiration. They are keen observers.

An older man wearing traditional Arab clothes is buying a falcon for himself. When we leave, we meet him again at his van as a young man is bringing him the falcon he has bought. The older man asks, "Are you falconers?" No, we say, but we love to watch the falcons fly. We are from New York. He says he belongs to the American Falcon Association! He was just in Denver at its meeting and he asks if we belong. We tell him no, but we love the falcons.

What a joyous way to end the trip to Qatar. Tomorrow we fly home.

CHAPTER 6

NEW YORK CITY

B̲arbara Journal:

March 19:

This morning Mr. Dependable takes me to the airport to catch an early flight to New York City where I will attend an Equinox gathering at the United Nations.

Few are on the road at 4:30 a.m. when Mr. Dependable picks me up, and we speed along without interruption. At the airport, I say good-bye, and enter the terminal to stand in line for Security inspection. My boarding pass has been printed out yesterday from the Internet, and I am ready to go.

Security is quick and easy and I am soon on my way to gate A5 to wait for my flight. Few are waiting here at this early hour, but a trickling soon begins, and by the time the plane is ready to be boarded, we have a full flight of passengers getting on.

It is cold this morning. Spring has forgotten to appear and so we are still dealing with winter. No snow has fallen for a couple days and the roadways are clear. The runways, as can be expected, are clear and the pilot has to deal with no problems. He takes us off the ground and I close my eyes and wait for the ride to end.

About halfway to New York City, I open my eyes to look out and I am surprised to see that below us is a heavy, unending mass of clouds! Does that mean we will have snow or rain for tomorrow's Equinox? I hope not!

As I am contemplating the worst, I begin to see bright orange-red color far out, at what seems to be the edge of the heavy cloud mass, and I know the sun has finished it's dark night and will appear. But, what is the famous saying? Red sun at night, sailor's delight. Red sun at morn, sailor take warn. The latter means those thick clouds I am looking at could come down to greet us today. OH DEAR!!!!

In any case, the pilot lands the plane and I am happy to note that the clouds seem to be staying upstairs rather then down here. Good! May they stay up there today, tomorrow, and the next few days.

I leave the plane wheeling my suitcase with my backpack where it should be, on my back, and I walk in the direction I hope will produce a sign saying I am heading toward Air Train. But there is no sign, and after a time, I ask for directions and discover that I have been walking in the wrong direction. Never mind. This has happened before. Everyone is friendly and helpful and eventually I reach Air Train and I take it to the Howard Beach stop and get off. Now I am ready for the next snag -- purchasing a metro ticket and putting ten rides on it.

Well, thank you, Higher Worlds. Just as I reach the metro ticket place, an attendant arrives and I tell him his timing is perfect because I am no good at figuring out what to do next. He straightens my coat collar which is being crushed by my back pack, and then he asks questions about what I want, etc., before beginning to push buttons and do all that is necessary here.

Interesting, when I am ready to leave and I am approaching the turnstile to put in my metro ticket, he is a bit behind me. He knows what is about to happen. I will insert my ticket upside-down, or whatever, and it won't work. He takes it from me, inserts it properly, the barrier opens and I go through.

Hurray! That's over! I give him a hearty good-bye and wish him an excellent day, and I go downstairs to wait for the C metro to take me into Manhattan.

This metro comes quickly and I, with a NYC map in my hand, watch the landscape pass by as we head toward Manhattan, cross the East River and begin to head steadily north to stops I recognize -- Chambers, 14th Street, 34th Street, etc. At Columbus Circle, I leave the C metro and search for the uptown Number 2 metro to take me to 96th Street, my final metro destination.

I soon learn that the Number 2 metro is Express and when I board, we race past a number of metro stops without pausing. In no time, I am at 96th Street and Broadway, and what is now needed is to climb stairs to Broadway, then walk to 94th Street, turn the corner and I am at my hotel, the Days Hotel Broadway.

SilverStar, called Grandmother because she is a Native American wise one, will be staying with me, and within a few minutes she has arrived. Another wise one called Gentle Bear has driven her and he will be coming every day from his home just outside New York City to drive us to various destinations.

Just now we are ready to go to the Cathedral of St. John the Divine only minutes from the hotel. We specifically are going here today because tomorrow is the great energy day of the Equinox. This place holds great energy for the Equinox as well as for the Solstice. I will not be here tomorrow and I want to touch base today so its energy will be included tomorrow when I am at the United Nations. Last June at the Solstice, an equally important energy day, I was at this cathedral during a Paul Winter event.

Today, when Gentle Bear has driven us to the cathedral, we see four or five big buses parked in front. Tourist buses. The cathedral is so big, many tourists could be inside but their number would seem diminished because of the size of the cathedral.

Inside, I am surprised to see that many of the pews have been removed. In fact, there are very, very few here. The remaining ones are near the altar, as one would expect.

We three, Grandmother SilverStar, Gentle Bear and I agree to meet near the altar in fifteen or twenty minutes, and I take my usual seat to meditate next to a towering column about thirty feet from the altar. To my left, high up on the wall, are French tapestries that seem new. I am thinking of the tapestries that were in danger of being damaged at a fire here just after the World Trade Center towers were brought down on September 11, 2001.

Firemen fighting the WTC fire rushed to the cathedral and afterward they left their signatures on a large white paper spread out on a huge tree stump table inside the cathedral. Today, March 19, I see the stump but the large paper with the names of the firefighters is no longer there.

At the far end of the cathedral, beyond the altar area, is a large stained glass window of the Christ wearing a red robe. At dawn last June, as the Solstice approached during the Paul Winter event, I watched the sun rising behind the stained glass window. It penetrated the window and brought out the bright red of his robe.

Today, when we leave the cathedral, it is time to think about our next stop, the River View room on the twenty-eighth floor of the NY Millennium Plaza Hotel more or less across the street from the big United Nations building. This afternoon, between the hours of two and four, we will attend a meeting of members of a UN non-governmental organization called the Committee on Sustainable Development, New York.

Today's meeting in this room is called "Middle Eastern Women: Taking the Lead on Sustainable Development", and there will be two main speakers, one from Oman and the other from Qatar. I have just visited Qatar, and even though I have never visited Oman, I have several times visited its next-door neighbor, the United Arab Emirates.

Our three names have been given to the meeting organizer, and when we arrive, we are warmly greeted. I will sit next to a woman from India and I am soon talking to her about her country. We eat as we talk because a buffet lunch has been provided. When the meeting is underway, everyone in the room is asked to stand and identify himself, or rather, herself. Most in the room are female. When those present identify their homelands, I am amazed that nearly all the world seems to be represented here. Egypt, China, India, the Middle East, U.S.A., etc.

The two speakers are excellent. The woman from Qatar, born in its capital, Doha, is today the Ambassador and Permanent Representative of Qatar at the United Nations. Throughout her speech, she remains optimistic about the advancement of the female in all aspects of Qatar. From my recent visit to Qatar, I think the female has a long way to go.

Today has been a long day, beginning very early, and when the meeting ends, I am ready to call it quits for the day. Tired!

March 20, EQUINOX:

The moment of the Spring Equinox is midday, 12:57 p.m., New York time, and we three will be at the United Nations for this important event that involves the ringing of a peace bell in the Rose Garden at the exact moment of the Spring Equinox, which is called the beginning of Earth Day, the renewal of the earth after winter. Years ago, John McConnell suggested this event here and the United Nations agreed. In 1998 he invited me to attend, and whenever possible, I have yearly attended. After the ringing, we all say "Happy Birthday, Mother Earth".

From experience I know we must dress warmly for this event, and I am happy that this year Mother Earth is holding off on harsh weather. Two years ago, I felt nearly frozen from wind coming off the East River only a few yards from the peace bell.

When I arrive today at the peace bell, eight young children holding violins are already gathered with their directress. Most are wearing light-colored formal dress and are without coats. Every year I love watching them vigorously playing their violins. And yes, their playing is vigorous. Their directress begins playing powerfully and they follow as best they can. If they are very young, they will have their bows perched on their violin strings, but they will not play if they are unable to keep up with the others.

Today, when all is ready at the peace bell, SilverStar and Gentle Bear open the ceremony singing a Native American song while SilverStar shakes a rattle and Gentle Bear taps on his drum. Then we pay tribute to legendary musician and environmentalist Pete Seeger who died a couple months ago and who rang the peace bell in 2009. Margaret and I not only attended this 2009 event, but a few years ago we also attended a gathering on the shores of the Hudson River to celebrate the cleaning of this river by Pete Seeger who used his boat called Clearwater.

As for today, I have brought with me large photographs of the Ugandan school children holding their gift of pencils at their school opening ceremony last month. They know we are at the United Nations for the ringing of the peace bell, and they are prepared to join us in thought. For them the exact moment of the Equinox will be in the evening and they will be in bed. We have suggested that they draw a peace bell they can take to bed with them and so in that way, they are with us! We want to join the 'very high' of the world, the United Nations, with the 'very low' of the world -- the children who have nothing. Today at the peace bell ringing ceremony I am invited to speak about these Ugandan children, and I am at the mike speaking and showing their photographs when the peace bell is struck! It is the exact moment of the Equinox!

Just before leaving for New York, I receive an email from Ruth of Uganda.

We are so glad Kasangula Talent is going to be represented at UN celebrations of Peace! Isn't this so wonderful, who has ever thought of such an opportunity to reach our children!! We want to thank you so much Barbara and Margaret for your great support and kindness to us. We are so grateful, we don't know how to thank you.

Ruth

After the ceremony, we three, SilverStar, Gentle Bear and I, are invited to attend a gathering at the United Nations of non-governmental organizations celebrating the International Day of Happiness. The idea behind this event is the belief that happiness is obtained when economies focus on social and environmental well-being.

We walk into the building following a United Nations affiliated person who 'opens doors for us' by swishing us past Security. Very soon we are entering a crowded dining area where many are standing in line to select food from a buffet. A check of all the tables reveals no unoccupied seats. There are purses on this chair and papers on another and brief cases and coats, etc. However, our friend who has brought us this far will not give up. She personally knows many in the room, and eventually three seats are found for us.

We are eating when the first speaker is at a mike and a video screen is near him to demonstrate his brief talk. Others follow him talking about their Happiness organizations, such as the Global Family and the Live Happy Media. These organizations cover a range of issues, including children's and women's rights, health, education, agriculture, climate change, etc. I am happy the United Nations is accepting these non-governmental organizations to help what is needed to be done in our world. One hears little about this.

March 21:

I label today as Wall Street Day. The money markets will be in full swing on Wall Street and I want the experience of being within this energy. Why? Money and those who control it are what makes the world go 'round. A few years ago protesters calling themselves the Occupy Wall Street movement were sitting on the doorsteps of the money markets of Wall Street. They said they had the energy of the

99 Percenters and the 1 Percenters were running the world. Many 99 Percenters waved their protest flags on Wall Street while the world news media clicked cameras. Soon the world was seeing:

BLAME WALL STREET GREED. WE ARE THE 99%.

WE DESERVE CHANGE! TAX THE 1%.

The movement began in 2011 in nearby Zuccotti Park, and as it grew in strength with massive demonstrations, Zuccotti Park was occupied. When the city's mayor said the park needed to be cleared for reasons of sanitation, 300,000 signed petitions opposing the eviction. Thousands began encircling the park and so the order to clear the park was cancelled.

Today I am in New York City, and yes, I want to see this place called Wall Street.

Metro 2 is a 'straight run' from its 96th Street stop to its Wall Street stop, and when I board the metro on 96th Street, I quickly realize that I am on an express metro that zooms me 'downtown' at a record rate! I am with Grandmother SilverStar, and soon we are leaving the metro train to walk in a tunnel with signs telling us where we should exit to reach specific city streets. But, where is the sign for Wall Street? We ask a passerby and he walks briskly ahead and then returns to tell us we should continue walking because there will be signs for Wall Street. And yes, there are signs and it turns out that Wall Street is the last street for this tunnel.

Above ground, we are at 40 Wall Street -- a number to remember later when we need to use the metro to leave Wall Street.

Our plan now is to walk to 80 Wall Street to meet Gentle Bear who has already sent a text to SilverStar's cell phone that he is waiting for us.

What is the feeling of Wall Street? Well, this morning is a dull morning with no sun. The tall city buildings here feel dull. Maybe the energies of creativity are hiding under a bench. We walk along, checking the street numbers until we reach number 80. Where is

Gentle Bear who is supposed to be waiting for us? SilverStar texts him on her cell phone and he answers he is at 40 Wall Street. What! We are at 80 and you are not!

A solution is quickly found. Thank you, cell phones! We will walk toward him and he will walk toward us. And yes, we meet at 60 Wall Street.

What is at 60 Wall Street? A large building open to the public called the Atrium. We enter this place and I am surprised to see a large expanse more or less empty except for a few card tables and places to sit. A few years ago, when the protest movement Occupy Wall Street was in full swing, the Atrium at 60 Wall Street was a major organizing place because public places cannot exclude people. It is only minutes away from Zuccotti Park where the protest movement began.

This morning when we are here, no meetings of any kind are within the walls of the Atrium. At one card table is a woman slumped over so that her body is occupying three-fourths of the table. She is fast asleep. Beside the table is a small baby carriage containing a large doll with a big head of hair. At first we think the doll is a child, but no. Is this doll representing the memory of her child? There is no baggage with the woman. My conclusion is that this woman is homeless and she is sleeping during the day in the Atrium because no one will send her away and no one will disturb her. During the night, does she have her hand out for money on a street corner? It is cold, very cold in New York. I shudder when I think of her nights in the cold.

We three have something for her, and I lightly tap her shoulder which wakes her. She raises her body off the card table and looks sleepily at me. She is about fifty-five and her face shows awful suffering. Will she live much longer? I do not think so. Will she welcome death? Maybe. There is nothing here for her. I place our gift on the table for her and we walk away.

Have we given her money? No. That was not even considered. What good is a bit of money? Her condition is beyond that. New York City has shown us those with conditions beyond that. They need BIG HELP and they will not get it.

Here is the background of our gift. Before arriving at Wall Street, one of the money capitals of the world which perhaps unintentionally tends to influence negative energies, to counter this, we have decided to leave something at Wall Street that has high, positive vibrations.

Flowers have high positive vibrations. The rose has one of the highest, and particularly the red rose. Yes! We will leave red roses!

Gentle Bear has bought three long-stemmed red roses before we found each other at 60 Wall Street. When we meet, he gives them to me and he shows us his finger which wears a bandage. He explains that when he is buying the roses, he accidently cuts his finger, and the flower seller graciously puts a bandage on the cut.

At Wall Street, we have no idea where we will put the red roses, but when we see the sleeping woman slumped over the card table, a pathetic doll in a small carriage beside her who could represent memories of her child, we know the roses will be for her.

Garbage containers are in the Atrium and I dig into one of them searching for a large paper cup used for drinking coffee by someone who could afford to buy a cup of coffee. Yes! There is a cup, and it is dry. Good!

We put the long stemmed red roses into the coffee cup, test it for balance and sturdiness, and then we put our gift on the card table for the woman and we walk away. Our hearts are satisfied.

Now we visit the nearby Zuccotti Park. There are no protest gatherings. Only a half dozen waiting to watch an acrobatic show by three colorfully dressed youth.

Now we are at the New York Stock Exchange and we continue walking without stopping. We walk past everything without stopping. Our thoughts now are on the World Trade Center only a short walk from Wall Street.

Many have the same idea to see the World Trade Center, and they are coming from all over the world. This scene is so different from when we came to the WTC after the September 11, 2001 disaster of the towers being deliberately struck by two jets. We arrived about two weeks afterward and firemen were still busy trying to put out fires. My thought then was that a lot of furniture in the downed towers was still burning.

In any case, when we visited in 2001, there were few pedestrians, so unlike today when there are many. Now, all want to visit this place that has become one of the most 'known' places in the world to visit.

We pass an old church with old gravestones bunched on a lawn in front of it. When the towers went down, this old cemetery was littered with paper coming from the towers, and much was still there when we arrived two weeks after the disaster.

Now we learn that we must have tickets to enter the fenced off WTC site. These are free tickets, but whoever wants to give a donation is perfectly welcome to do this. We follow signs to the ticket place located inside a building and then we stand in line waiting our turn. The ticket man is a young male in his early twenties, and he is patient and friendly. I am wondering how many days he has passed out tickets. Certainly, if he has been doing this long, his smile would be wiped off now from his face.

After we have our tickets in our hand, we wait in a long line to enter the fenced off World Trade Center grounds. This line is near McDonald's, which probably has a big business all day long rather than just during normal mealtimes. Actually, there are several lines waiting to enter the fenced off World Trade Center grounds. We pick the line that, hopefully will be the fastest.

Well, there is no sense being impatient because this will not help. We wait for a time and then our line moves a bit, giving us hope for a moment before it stops. This is the routine until we are finally inside the fenced off area of the World Trade Center and we can wander as we please, with plenty of space for everyone to do the same.

We approach one of two big pools of water with artificial falls, and we think this is where the two main towers used to stand. The names of firemen and their particular engine numbers are placed on a wall overlooking the big pools, and I think these are the fire fighters who died here.

One thing I remember when visiting in 2001, people would come with written prayers in their hands to give to firemen who would post them on a big wooden cross near the fire.

How does this place called the World Trade Center feel today? Not good. The energies of horror are still here. Many, many died here. Some chose to jump out of high-storey windows; others were trapped in elevators; others died on stairs. Breathing was terrible during the ordeal, and inhalation of poisoned air killed many. Later, more died from what they had inhaled.

The people here today looking at the tragic site know what they are looking at and they were somber. When they finish looking, they were still somber as they leave the place. I think most would feel comfortable giving something. I think a small, artificial pool should be built inside the fenced area with a sign saying that anyone wishing to give from their hearts a few coins to a child whose father has been killed fighting the fires should place the coins in the artificial pool. There could be a small birdhouse structure for money other than coins. I think that if visitors can give a small token from their hearts, they would feel they have helped here.

When I return home, I send this idea to the New York government in Albany.

March 23, Brooklyn:

Today, Sunday, is a Big Day -- listening to the Brooklyn Tabernacle choir. We are excited to go. Grandmother SilverStar and I leave our hotel about 8 a.m. and we are soon at the 96th Street metro line Number 2 to take a quick journey to nearly the doorstep of the tabernacle.

But, because the day is Sunday, which means it is the weekend and time for metros to be repaired, or whatever, we wait and we wait and we wait for Metro 2, and it is slow coming. A public announcement over a loudspeaker tells us that the rails for Metro 2 are closed just now, but this is temporary.

We wait.

Finally, Metro 2 comes and we board. Many are already on it and seats are limited, but we find two places to sit.

And yes, Metro 2 speeds along, making few stops before it reaches Hoyt, our destination. We climb the stairs, ask directions to the tabernacle, receive them, walk briskly, and when we realize a number of people are turning right ahead of us, we also turn and walk along, following the people. They seem to know where they are going, and they are being quick about walking, as if they will risk being late. We know it is time for the tabernacle choir to begin singing and we also walk briskly.

But now there is a problem. Gentle Bear has texted SilverStar's cell phone to say he is at the entrance waiting for us, but, where is he? We are at the door to the tabernacle and he is not here. SilverStar texts him and he answers back immediately that he is at the door.

What shall we do?

I leave SilverStar outside waiting for him and I enter the tabernacle and meet volunteers wanting to direct me to a place to sit. I poke my head into the huge source of singing and see a big stage with a choir wearing colorful dress facing a huge audience. The place is packed and the audience is singing full out with the choir. WOW! What shall we do? Join the singing or wait for Gentle Bear to come from wherever he may be?

After a short time, I return to SilverStar waiting outside and we make the decision to join the singing. But the place is packed! Where can we sit? Never mind. Volunteers are used to finding seats for latecomers and we are directed to seats near the back. Those already there squeeze together to make room for us. At the moment, the audience is standing and singing and we join them. A small, overhead TV screen gives us the gospel words to sing. When it ends, another begins and then another and another. WONDERFUL.

THE LOVE POWER POURING FROM THEIR HEARTS IS ENORMOUS.

When we do sit and a pastor begins speaking to us, I learn the number of all of us singing together is probably 2000!

After a time, who should appear but Gentle Bear. A volunteer is directing him to sit only two rows ahead of SilverStar and me. I think, how incredible it is for him to be seated just ahead of us when there are 2000 here. Later, when we three join, I learn he has told the seating volunteer that he is supposed to be with ladies who have entered the tabernacle about fifteen minutes earlier. The volunteer says she knows this and she seats him as close as she can to us. Amazing!

After the service, Gentle Bear says he has gone to the Brooklyn Tabernacle Church to wait for us, and after a time he realizes he is meeting us at the wrong place!

Now the pastor on stage, with a colorful choir of probably 200 behind him, asks us 2000 seated in front of him, to shake hands with our neighbors, and we stand again and do this. Fun!

He begins telling us he has just returned from Hong Kong where he was invited to speak. He says close to two million live there as Christians, which comes as a surprise to me. Are they all Chinese? I think there is probably a mixture of races.

In any case, the pastor, when he arrives in Hong Kong, realizes he is to speak every day at many difference places, one right after the other. About eleven hours a day. He is given interpreters who wear out, but he has to keep going.

When the morning's program is finished, the audience is invited to eat in a dining area and we three are in favor of doing this. We file downstairs with others and select an assortment of food offered at a very low price.

After experiencing the tabernacle, one feels tempted to relocate to Brooklyn to live close by.

There is a P.S. to this tabernacle experience.

Later, Margaret and l listen on the Internet to the Brooklyn Tabernacle chorus and all the people singing. IT IS MIGHTY POWERFUL to listen to this singing, to feel this positive love energy. We sent it to Mother Earth.

CHAPTER 7

INDIAN POINT NUCLEAR POWER PLANT

J oint Journals:

From Barbara:

In early March, the Higher Worlds unexpectedly say to me: *"These are the last days of Pompeii. Enjoy yourself."*

This is a surprise! Why have they mentioned Pompeii? I have not been thinking of Pompeii. Not even thinking of Italy, and yet, here is such a statement coming from the Higher Worlds.

After some pondering, I suddenly realize the meaning: Pompeii stands for New York City, less than forty miles from the Indian Point Nuclear Power Plant, ready to be destroyed by a catastrophic earthquake. Obviously, the work is to stop this catastrophe from happening.

I speak with Margaret, and one thing leads to another and I realize that this earthquake is ready to happen now. NOW. NOW. NOW.

We begin playing sacred Musical Rapture and we both go into meditation. I 'look' at the two fault lines on which the Indian Point Nuclear Power Plant is sitting, and I do not feel the energy field is unusually powerful. Yet, I know that forces within Mother Earth can drive up power here. Therefore, one needs to ACT NOW.

What can I do?

Over the area of Fukushima, I have been helping to strengthen an esoteric pyramid with a capstone being fed unique Love energy coming from the Higher Worlds. This unique Love energy cannot attract negative energy.

I decide to copy the Fukushima work by putting an esoteric pyramid capstone over the area of the Indian Point Nuclear Power Plant, and yes, this is easy enough to do. I work with the 'unseen' ones whose homes are within Mother Earth. They know me and I know them. One time I was in the Crystal Cave in the Black Hills, and when the 'unseen' ones and I met in their homeland, the energy was so powerful, it blew out the electric lights in the cave as well as my flashlight which never recovered even when new batteries were put in.

Yes, the 'unseen' ones are mighty, mighty powerful, and today, at the intersection of the two fault lines at Indian Point, they are there with me as I reduce the energy within Mother Earth to diminish the chance of an earthquake. When I finish, I am satisfied.

I know the Law of Cause and Effect. Thought has energy. What one thinks has an effect. Stop the pressure of the two fault lines and there is less chance of disruption at the Indian Point Nuclear Power Plant. Hence, no new Pompeii.

When I finished, I feel a sense of good, a sense of having done the proper thing.

However, I know more work needs to be done. This power plant needs to be closed down. It is too close to New York City. If it is damaged by an earthquake, think of the millions living there who would either have to leave or stay and take in powerful radiation.

I write to Governor Andrew Cuomo, head of New York State, to tell him that we support his desire that the nuclear power plant be closed down. He is the head one, and by writing a brief letter to him, we put our energies with he who wishes that the power plant be closed down.

From Margaret:

On a map showing the Indian Point Power Plant on the Hudson River in New York State, I place the Vortexes and three large healing crystals. Also, an article about the potential danger of an earthquake at this location. I am ready.

I go into meditation to help stop an earthquake. I connect to the Dolphins in Hawaii to collect their energy. Together we go to the Council of the Brothers and Sisters of the Higher Worlds and ask for Earth stability in the Indian Point Nuclear Power Plant area. Immediately a strong announcement is made: *The fault is not at fault!* I feel tension lessen in the fault lines. One sentence, gentle humor, soothes the fracture. The Dolphins swim in the fault lines, smoothing gently, with movement and balance. Softly, gently, making watery the rock fault lines that energetically are no longer rigid!

The softness of a Dolphin's Smile reflects the Divine Love Music playing for the meditation.

I am given a strong symbol from the Brothers and Sisters of the Higher Worlds, two large angle points merging into each other with an intersecting line locking them. This is a gift reflecting stability and balance for Mother Earth.

I feel great peace. The crisis is over.

When the meditation ends, both Barbara and I feel a sense of relief.

March 22, from Barbara:

The Indian Point meditation was a couple weeks ago and now I am in New York City with Gentle Bear driving me and SilverStar to the

Indian Point Nuclear Power Plant. I am riding along thinking about the words of the Higher Worlds, "These are the last days of Pompeii. Enjoy yourself." When we realize they were talking about New York City, Margaret and I went to work to stop an earthquake. Now I am going to Indian Point.

It is cold today as we drive along, but at least there is no snow, a blessing.

The vicinity of Indian Point is easily reached, but now our maps become vague as to the actual location of the nuclear power plant. When we slow our pace to ask passersby, we are greeted with polite but vague answers. The response tells us that some residents are nervous about directing us to the place.

We go along slowly, using our intuition to drive near the water which we think the nuclear power plant requires. Now we see domes very close to the road. The area is blocked for traffic, but we are on a public road parallel to the plant. My thought is that this place is too close to local residences. It is as if the local residents must live with the nuclear power plant in their backyards!

Yes, too close. Much too close. That is my opinion.

When we leave the area, we see a sign at a bus stop indicating that buses stop here for forced evacuations. I think it is unfair to have this plant so close to the people who live here. Would I want my children to be brought up under such circumstances?

I note that Indian Point and its surroundings have a comfortable energy field. People like to live here. I would like to live here if there is no nuclear threat.

When I return home, I check the Internet for remarks on Indian Point and I read that 2.5 billion gallons of water are used daily to keep generators cool. Fish are sucked into the water with a consequence of a billion fish and other water organisms being killed every year. Can the consciousness dismiss this as nothing? My consciousness cannot.

CHAPTER 8

HEALER BRACO

J oint Journals:

From Barbara:

In 2011, while in Istanbul attending an annual November 1 celebration of the World Brotherhood Union, I unexpectedly hear the name Braco, a Croatian whose fame for healing has been increasing world wide. Angelika Whitecliff, a panelist living in Hawaii, speaks about him, as does Dr. Michael Salla, another panelist.

I am yearly invited to attend the Istanbul conference because I am a panelist advisor and a former panelist. I eat meals with them, and even sightsee with them at famous places including the spice market. I was at the spice market when Angelika Whitecliff and Michael Salla bought a very large pink metal suitcase. Was it for Braco?

A few weeks later, while attending a Native American gathering in Cahokia, Illinois, Margaret and I meet Carmen Balhestero, who over the years has invited us to speak at her Peace Center outside Sao Paulo, Brazil. We offer to take her sightseeing around Washington, D.C. before taking her to a Braco gazing healing session near the capital. His recent arrival and a chance to see him excites Carmen and us!

And so, we three go to a large auditorium seating about three hundred to see Braco gazing. We watch as he enters the room and walks to a podium to stand and begin gazing for about eight minutes.

The audience watches him silently. There is not even a cough or a sneeze. All attention is on him. His face wears a slight smile, and, as if timed, he slowly moves his head a bit to the right and then to the left for the benefit of the audience. The intense concentration on him makes one tingle.

I have read many comments about the gazing. Some are healed; others feel better; many feel great peace.

Volunteers are always present during the gazing sessions, ready to support those in the audience whose reaction to Braco's energy is too much. They collapse. Braco does not proclaim himself to be a healer even though a great many suffering from disease, including cancer, have claimed to be cured.

He travels the world with thousands coming to his gazing sessions. In 2012 his travels took him to the church center of the United Nations in New York City. During this session, he was presented with a peace pole by the World Peace Prayer Society to honor him for peace efforts. I cannot confirm this, but afterwards his photograph with the peace pole was shown at Times Square, and police officials reported afterwards less crime in the area,

As for myself, when I am attending the gazing session near Washington, I feel intense energy produced by the audience uniting with the energy of Braco. The energy of peace and healing.

This past June Braco was in New York City to do gazing sessions. From there, he made a brief visit to Niagara Falls and then he went to Rochester, New York, where I attended a gazing session.

I arrive a few minutes early and line up with others at an auditorium door waiting for volunteers in an orderly manner to usher us in and seat us. Before entering, while in line waiting, in front of me is a very tall thin black-haired male wearing black clothes. I do not know his nationality, but my thought is he is Russian. When the auditorium door opens and we begin filing in, I see that this male is so badly crippled, it is amazing to me that he is able to walk. Is this condition the result of a motorcycle accident or from war? My thought is that if Braco's gazing can heal him, anyone can be healed.

When we are seated in the auditorium, I am about fifteen rows from the platform where Braco will be standing. I look at the audience. Some are wearing around their necks photographs of their children and others. Braco has asked that photographs come for those who cannot physically be here. In the audience, I see unaccompanied, white-haired men in wheelchairs, looking pudgy. Have they been eating meat laced with hormones? How many of them have diabetes? All have the intense look of wanting Braco's gaze to help them. A woman sitting beside me has her eyes closed and is in a meditative state throughout the gazing. Will she look at Braco or remain in mediation with her eyes closed?

When Braco arrives, he walks to the stage in front of us to begin gazing. The concentration of the audience is intense. I see a circle of light behind him. It is an amazing experience.

In June, for over a week, a wealthy, elderly woman in Switzerland has donated money so the world can freely see Braco gazing on the Internet. There is even a film of him speaking in Croatian. Margaret and watch him on the Internet and we hope these sessions will continue. This is the world coming together with thoughts of peace and healing. The computer is being used to unite the world via Braco.

From Margaret:

On the Internet, I am watching Braco gazing from Croatia.

June 13:

2:20 p.m., when I watch the gazing of Braco, I see the blue gold of the sea behind him in Croatia. He is robust and full of joy which he transfers to the viewers. Joy spreads all around. The White Light of his aura spreads. No wonder people bring children and flowers to him. They are full of Joy.

3:30 p.m., it feels like the Sun is coming out when Braco looks directly at me. Enclosed within his gaze is all of Mother Earth, and a feeling of the Sun in its movement and intensity. Joy and life are transmitted with his direct gaze.

4:40 p.m., direct gazing. Direct eye to eye, heart to heart, acknowledging each other. Gazing makes space for everyone in the world. Deep joy. Deep gratitude. Deep connection. Unification of all humanity by love.

5:20 p.m., again, direct gazing. Enthusiasm. I feel we are in front of a grand cathedral and Braco is looking at me and seeing my guardian guides, angels, ancestors, descendants. All in a great space around me.

He looks to all of them and we are all together in this love gaze that feels like a warm fire. Every aspect in one's life is seen in the gazing.

My terrible headache washes away. It evaporates, moves off like a passing storm on the horizon.

The Sun comes out and the storm (headache) disappears.

Thank you, Braco.

June 14:

A message given while Braco is gazing: *Nature is Source. Be close to Nature. Be close to Source.*

When receiving Braco's gazing, I feel we are all facing the Sun, a cascading waterfall of love.

I receive: *Open the door and smile. Smile brings healing. You smile, the world smiles. The sea smiles. The people smile. A smile is the signal of love – the sun sign.*

Today is the last day of gazing sessions on the Internet. It is announced that there have been 225,000 computers in 81 countries tuned to Braco's gazing sessions. Peace has spread around the world. This echoes the November 26, 2012 miracle on Times Square, when a big screen in Times Square three times shows Braco receiving the gift of a peace pole from the World Peace Prayer Society at the United Nations for his work for world peace. The screen posted the words, "Braco Shares His Special Gift for World Peace with the United Nations." The next day, the news reported that for first time in the memory of New York City there was no crime in the city for the entire day. May Peace Prevail On Earth.

June 24:

Braco comes to Rochester, New York to gaze. I have helped send out announcements. Before he comes to Rochester, he goes to Niagara Falls, a great energy power place for the world. A photograph of him at the falls is posted on the Internet. The power is awesome.

This afternoon, a taxi comes to take me to the Plaza Hotel where Braco will gaze for two days. I am a volunteer and all volunteers must attend a 3:00 p.m. meeting with the key organizers. I meet the volunteers who are excellent. We are shown the ballroom that has 370 chairs for tonight's event called 'Living Peace.'

As a volunteer, I am asked to be a doorkeeper, and this evening, when the people arrive, I greet each one wishing them a joyful evening. More and more keep arriving. More chairs are needed. We find them and when the program begins at 7:30 p.m., 430 people are seated.

The program features a full line of musicians and speakers to celebrate peace and Braco's gazing. A Native American flute player opens the ceremony and then others are soon playing pianos, the vibraphone, the guitar, and the violins. Singers sing their original compositions. We audience bask in a delight of listening to soaring peace songs and love songs.

When Braco begins gazing for the audience, they watch him intently, taking in his powerful healing energy. When the program ends, all receive a Braco video.

Today there has been a great rainstorm and the sun then came out and a rainbow appeared over the hotel. Someone took a photograph. Later I saw it on the Internet. WOW! Perfect.

June 25:

In the morning I return to the Plaza Hotel to attend two meetings for volunteers. Over 50 are here, and all are enthusiastic. I am assigned to greet people and tell them which desk to go to for tickets. There are two types of tickets – one for a single session and one for an all day session. The day goes smoothly. From time to time, with the agreement of the supervisors, I am permitted to slip in to see the gazing.

As the two-day event progresses, I feel the gazing sessions are growing stronger and stronger. At the last session, Braco's voice is played, and then, when everyone is leaving, flowers are passed out. I think about the times on the Internet when I have seen flowers passed out to the people on leaving gazing sessions. They bring flowers to him and when the gazing is over, he returns the flowers with a blessing.

CHAPTER 9

STAR KNOWLEDGE CONFERENCE, NASHVILLE, TENNESSEE

Joint Journals:

Barbara Journal:

September 16, our favorite taxi driver takes us to the airport to catch a flight to New York City. We intend to go to Nashville, Tennessee, to attend a conference, but we want to stay overnight in New York City before flying there. However, when we try to book a NYC hotel room, to our surprise, the city is stuffed with people. At the United Nations, world leaders, including President Obama, are gathering and this has resulted in hotels not being available. We must look elsewhere and we find a hotel nearly across the street from the Newark airport in New Jersey.

On arrival in NYC, it is easy enough to reach the Newark airport by taking the subway to Penn Station. Here, we buy a New Jersey Transit ticket to take us to Newark where we transfer to a little Air-Train consisting of four or five small cars and no driver. Instructions for passengers come over a loud speaker. We jump aboard and sit with others going to the airport. On arrival, we get off at a busy terminal to phone for a free shuttle to take us to the Holiday Inn where we will stay overnight. Within minutes, a shuttle driver picks us up and takes us nearly next door to the hotel. We are impressed with this hotel. It is modern, clean and every aspect gives attention to comfort.

September 17:

Our flight today takes us to Nashville's airport where a rental car is ready for us. It is shiny black and a new model. We must be careful to put no dents in this new car! With Margaret driving and I in the passenger seat holding Google maps, we begin about a thirty-five mile drive to Montgomery Bell State Park to attend a three-day gathering called Star Knowledge Conference, Nashville, The Great Thanksgiving.

The Native American calendar called the EarthStar Way Calendar, lists eight special moments to celebrate the bringing in and anchoring of Cosmic Light for Mother Earth. One of the eight ceremonies is called the Ceremony of Thanksgiving. The Nashville conference comes at this moment when it is respected. Hence, The Great Thanksgiving becomes the name of the conference. Lightworkers who gather here will be enhancing the Cosmic Light coming in for Mother Earth.

Please check the Glossary on how to access this calendar.

We drive out of the airport rental car building and begin following signs to 40 West, an expressway jammed with cars and trucks. Hundreds are moving between 25 and 40 miles per hour. No one seems anxious, which, to my mind, means this is a usual occurrence. Oh dear! This city, so famous for its country music, should have loud speakers along 40 West to entertain drivers as they crawl along.

When we reach Exit 188 we turn off the expressway to travel on Rt. 247, but now the Google instructions I have in my hand are unclear and we soon feel lost. We are in a rural area with few shops, but there are enough so one can stop and ask for directions. This turns out to be fun. We stop and I jump out of our little rental car to explain we are lost. The immediate reaction is kind and courteous with an eagerness to help. Yes, it is fun being lost.

We only have to stop three times, and the third inquiry brings a deep Southern accent. I have to listen carefully to grasp the meaning of some words. For example, I am told we should go straight ahead and not turn left or right and we will come to a big heel. Heel? The heel of a foot? What does this mean? I don't want to ask him because it would be impolite. Oh! I understand. The word is Hill. He is talking about a hill. Yes, it is fun being lost. Maybe we need to keep getting lost.

In any case, we do reach the Montgomery Bell State Park, and a two-mile drive inside this heavily wooded place takes us to the combined conference/hotel building where we will stay.

Our room faces a manmade pond, or lake, as the locals call it, made during the Depression. All lakes in this park are manmade, we are told, and this is a huge park. In the evening, below our room, geese arrive to peck the grass. When the light fades, they move to the water to float for protection from predators.

Interesting, when one takes the elevator to reach our room, the lobby is marked as being on the fourth floor, not the first floor. Our room, when using the elevator, is on the third floor. Can you image the confusion we have when we first use the elevator? Whoever heard of going up to reach the lobby and going down to reach rooms that overlook a lake?

Well, our thoughts are soon focused on the conference. We are happy to see the headman, Chief Golden Light Eagle, who is wearing full Native American regalia. We are also happy to see another friend, Grandmother SilverStar, and she introduces us to her friends, many of whom are from the Nashville area. We meet Chandra and her mother and Bearcloud. On the second day, we have a cellphone message from a Japanese friend who says he will soon arrive. The people attending this conference are Lightworkers and each has his own specialty. Three hundred are brought together here. A blending of Light energy for the world.

Actually, there is a second reason why we are here. The Native American conference is located at the heart of important mound country, and close by there is a mound called Mound Bottom, considered to be one of the most important mounds in this area.

Even though a large number of mounds are found throughout North America, and they have been here a long time, it is curious to me that the mounds have not caught the attention of most residents living in North America.

Who has built these mounds? Frank Joseph will tell you. He has written a book, Advanced Civilizations of Historic America. The cover of his book also includes the words: The Lost Kingdoms of the Adena, Hopewell, Mississippians, and Anasazi. Yes, Frank Joseph will tell you his interpretation of the people who lived here and built these mounds.

We have been taught to think that only Native Americans we call Indians lived here before the White Man arrived. Evidence, including the many mounds, shows that others lived here earlier. Some lived here thousands of years ago. At Cahokia, Illinois, mounds were built by Mayans who came up from the Yucatan, and eventually the population may have reached 200,000. An elaborate complex of mounds was built there for ceremonial and other purposes. One mound, Monks Mound, remains today as a major mound at Cahokia and this seems to have a link with Mound Bottom near Nashville.

For some reason, at a certain time everyone left Mound Bottom, as they did at Cahokia. Frank Joseph says in his book that a main priest had the authority to tell people they must leave and the people obeyed.

Of interest to me is that people -- men, women and children – were sacrificed at ancient mounds. Some had their heads cut off and some had their hands cut off. Were these sacrificed ones ready to leave the earth? Would they be caught in bardo between the 3D earth and the next dimension? If so, they probably will remain until they are released.

A few years ago Margaret and I were in Hiroshima and unexpectedly the Higher Worlds told us to release those caught. We 'opened the door' and, we are told over 144,000 left. We don't expect that many to be caught in the Nashville area but we have need to release whoever is caught. Specifically, we are thinking of the souls. Mother Earth has already ascended to a higher dimension and we are supposed to ascend, too. Those in bardo, can they ascend? We think not without help.

Attending the Nashville conference gives us a chance to think about this release because, on September 21, Sunday, we conference people are invited to go to Mound Bottom to do ceremony. This will be a powerful gathering of Lightworkers. However, releasing those in bardo require a certain amount of stillness and meditation. We will not have these two requirements. We realize we cannot join the September 22 Mound Bottom ceremony.

There is one more matter to consider. I have asked the Global Meditations Network people to send prayers for the September 21 Mound Bottom ceremony, and many prayers have been sent to Nashville. SilverStar has agreed to take the prayers to the Mound Bottom ceremony, and so that problem has been solved.

What will we be doing on September 21, also called the International Day of Peace? A few days ago, we were invited to be a part of a global teleconference on that day. Specific people around the world will be saying a word or two, and a moment will be set aside for meditation and the giving out of the universal message of May Peace Prevail On Earth. The purpose is to activate an existing peace pole grid consisting of over 200,000 peace poles already planted throughout the world. Those who participate will be performing a powerful act of planetary acupuncture by sending energy to all the peace poles around the planet for a global attunement for peace. Those who cannot be on the telephone are asked to gather around a peace pole at that time or plant one. Yes, on September 21, we will join world Lightworkers on a teleconference and we will do this at a hotel near the airport.

September 21:

We leave the conference hotel at the Montgomery Bell State Park to drive to the airport to return our little rental car that has been very good to us. We have given it no dents. Traffic is light today, Sunday morning, and there are few trucks. Instead of crawling along at 25 miles per hour, we race and we are quickly at the airport to turn in our car. A free shuttle then takes us a short way to the Holiday Inn Express where we are given a room. When we ask about the availability of a telephone that will join us successfully to the global teleconference, the manager is very obliging. He shows us the hotel's boardroom where we can use a telephone he guarantees will do the job. And yes, the telephone does work perfectly. We connect for nearly two hours with the world of global Lightworkers.

Only for a moment are we disappointed. Our friend living in Japan fails to speak when it is his turn. Why? Has his phone been disconnected? We are happy the conference organizers do not forget him, and a while later, they try again to reach him. Yes. His voice comes through loud and clear!

September 22:

When we are at the Nashville airport waiting for our plane, we enjoy watching youth carrying cased guitars, flutes, etc. We know they have come to Nashville because this is the headquarters of country music. We can imagine how much good country music they have listened to during their visit here! Probably some of them were able to play their instruments with others. The next time we come to Nashville we will listen to the wonderful country music.

Margaret Journal:

In the summer, July 29, I am channeling Yolanda of the Pleiades:

Dear Yolanda, September 18 - 21, near Nashville, Tennessee, at Montgomery Bell State Park, there will be a big gathering called Star Knowledge Conference Nashville The Great Thanksgiving. We are told there will be a big gathering of star fleets.

We are deciding whether or not to go. What is your opinion? What is the importance? The area has ancient mounds. What is the significance of the mounds? Does this gathering have any connection to Athena, ancient Greek Goddess of Wisdom? The people of Nashville have built a modern Parthenon, Temple to her. Does this have anything to do with the conference?

Answer: This is an important gathering on many levels. Roads are being opened, bridges built, old structures (mounds) energy lines activated. The consciousness of all the people is being raised. With the waking up of the people, the land becomes alive again. Dormant currents are activated.

The energies spread outward, energizing the planet, enlivening peace, joy and harmony.

Energies spread upwards joining life forms on planet and off planet. A conference on many levels with many systems and frequencies and homelands attending.

The Past Earth is coming forward to join the Future Earth. Joining, intermingling, energizing the people with contact and wisdom in a peaceful, hospitable way. It is the generosity of Spirit through the expression of The Great Thanksgiving that all is witnessed, shared and honored. Quiet is the dawn. All are assembled and hearts are joined in Peace and Love. Open the door. Come. Come. Come to the gathering. Lives, Wisdom, Understandings will be shared. Books will be opened.

With warmest Greetings,

Yolanda

To prepare for the trip we research the Montgomery Bell State Park and the nearby mounds, especially nearby Mound Bottom where there will be a September 21 Fall Equinox sunrise ceremony.

I ask, can someone comment on the September 21 pre-dawn gathering at Mound Bottom?

The Council of Light answers: A gathering with strong intent will create a mighty force field to enliven the place, the time, and the gatherers. Each holds a significant role.

The Native Americans are the record keepers, calendar holders and teachers. They are the receivers and distributors.

The others attending are receivers and distributors of energy for the planet.

Attendees from other homelands will gather to contact, energize, strengthen and honor Mother Earth for her service. The unification of force fields will enhance Mother Earth's balance and harmony.

The Equinox – a sacred time for all.

I remember David Adams from Australia telling us we will have visitors from other worlds that will give us knowledge if we open our hearts and minds to them.

When I think of this I feel energy rising and I ask: "How do we prepare for the fleets?

Answer: Clean your house. From the mind, get rid of unwanted debris. Fix your fences. Open the gates. Open your hearts. Be prepared to sing a welcome song. Birds sing a chorus at each new day. Sing a welcome song.

Lighten your hearts. Lighten your minds.

Separation between peoples needs to be diminished and will be diminished in the gathering of people from different homelands.

The language is through the heart. The mind divides. The heart embraces. The strangers are no longer. Long distance relatives reunited. A grand family reunion. Stay tuned, dear Margaret. Music is on the wind. We can feel your excitement, uplift-ment.

I add, maybe this could stop the fighting here on planet Earth.

Answer: May be. Maybe.

August 1, more channeling:

I note birds are visiting Chief Golden Light Eagle with messages. Barbara keeps seeing pale yellow birds flying close to the window. What are their messages?

I ask the Bird Kingdom, do you have a message for me?

Blue Bird speaks: Birds indicate their messages by their gestures. They come close when they want to make contact. Large birds, hawks and eagles, fly circles or swoops to honor or to support. Little birds come close to transfer wisdom or give observations.

Birds fly. Birds walk. Birds see the environment from another perspective. Trees, flowers, air, water are important to the birds. Their habitat needs to be welcoming. Pollution and radiation diminish the population. Humans need to be mindful of the state of the birds. They are allies. They are mind readers. Faster than you can think, they have passed you by before you noticed.

Remember the sweet robin that walked with you at the reservoir, the hawk that circled, the eagle that flew over Barbara. Birds are in the trees singing their chorus. They are there to lift the Spirit ... for you ... for Mother Earth. Listen. Stay tuned.

I don't understand exactly why the birds wanted to comment. I do know that Chief Golden Light Eagle who is the focus of the Nashville Conference has been visited by birds, eagles. I know that if this conference is a success, much energy will be given to Mother Earth and all that live on her, including the birds. I know they must suffer because of pollution brought on by the actions of humans. To stop the pollution would be a great asset to them.

September 16:

We are riding a taxi to the airport, speaking with the taxi driver who loves Nashville's country music. We won't have time for country music but we will return to visit the Grand Ole Opry.

This morning, we take a flight to JFK and then the subway to Penn Station where we have breakfast at a delicatessen to eat good food. We are perched on high stools around a small circular table when Barbara's fork flies to the floor. A kind young man sitting beside us quickly retrieves a new fork and gives it to her. We are touched by his thoughtfulness.

The mood here in Penn Station is somber with tight Security, and the actions of this kind young man are quite the opposite. Why is the mood so somber today? Probably it has to do with the ongoing attacks in the Middle East. From Penn Station we take a train to Newark, New Jersey, and then an Air Train to the airport. When we reach the airport, we take a shuttle to the Holiday Inn where we stay the night.

September 17:

This morning we take a flight to Nashville in a tiny plane, a miniature compared to the big modern airport where we arrive. Our concentration is on renting a car and we stop at Enterprise where we receive help picking out a car, a new and simple one. An attendant waits patiently while I try all the knobs and turn signals. She sets the lights on permanent setting. Good.

As we drive slowly to Montgomery Bell State Park, site of the conference, we are caught in a big traffic jam moving at 25 miles per hour. We move so slowly, we have time to note that the rock cliffs beside the highway are similar to the Niagara Escarpment further north. Here are deep and high and powerful, amazing rock layers!

As I drive along, with my mind, I erase the traffic jam and the modern buildings of the present and visualize the past during the time of the mound builders when all was clean, strong and green with big trees.

When we do arrive at the Montgomery Bell State Park entrance, having been lost a couple times, a white car pulls in ahead of us and stops. We stop, too. It is SilverStar! She has been driving for three days and we have been flying for two days and we meet at the entrance to the park. Coincidence?

In the soft afternoon light, we drive together through the green cathedral of trees reaching over the road. What a glory! Our destination, the Inn, site of the conference and our hotel, is at least a two-mile drive in this gorgeous park. When we arrive, we check in and are given accommodations.

September 18:

I sit with Barbara and listen to all the speakers, one right after the other. When each speaker goes to the podium, four men drum and sing as an introduction in a Native American way. It is an honoring.

Particularly, I am interested in a lecture by Thomas Johnson, who can communicate with ancient fossils. They show him where they are, and he carefully removes them from rocks where they are embedded. After the lecture, I speak with Thomas Johnson and he tells me how Kirlian photography captures the essence of the powerful energy of the sharp spikes of the fossils. He says the whole energy field remains intact even if there are damaged or missing pieces.

When Grandma Chandra conducts a healing journey in her workshop, I meditate and see the green cathedral of trees arching over the road. This scene becomes a real cathedral with tall pillars and arches supporting a decorative ceiling.

While still in meditation, I go beyond the cathedral to an open space, an angelic field, realm of the Angels where one can feel joy and new beginnings. This can serve as a prototype for the souls of the Mound Bottom people who were sacrificed and in bardo.

After the meditation, SilverStar invites Barbara and me to speak at her workshop because she wants us to talk about placing Vortexes around the world. Those attending listen attentively and take all our books.

September 21:

When the conference is over and the teleconference is over, we want to rest poolside in a garden connected to the hotel. But, contrary to our thoughts, rest will not happen. A young girl about eight years old is having continual tantrums. She is shrieking and screaming and twisting her body here and there. Her parents are with her and they seem to be used to these outbursts. They have given up trying to stop her.

What I am seeing is a shock to me after having attended such high level events. I channel to ask why is the child suffering. Is it the food? Is it the frequencies?

Answer: She needs the love, devotion of animals who connect her with Mother Earth. Too much noise. Too much electricity.

The child needs space. She needs affirmation. Maybe dance, art, music.

I draw on my notebook the Symbols of Love and Healing and the Symbol for the Protection of the Family.

Later in the afternoon, I watch the vibrant clouds above me. They look like dragons and a heart. They feel like ships. I greet my Brothers and Sisters and I project their grand love over Mother Earth. The worlds are coming closer together.

In the evening while I am doing my exercises, I ask the bardo people to exercise with me. This involves joining the golden sun with the silver moon and the universe to form the energy as electrical currents that make a golden staircase and a silver staircase for the Mound Bottom people to ascend.

September 22:

In the night, I have terrible nightmares and I wake with unrest. I hold the Vortex Symbols and speak their names. I use them to polish the surfaces of my mind.

I channel asking what is the meaning of this.

Emma Kunz answers: You have been living in the 11th dimension at Montgomery Bell State Park. That is why you cannot comprehend a nightmare. That is why it was such a shock to come to the hotel pool and you see the disjointed frantic child who suffers from the toxic poison of TV and all disjointed matter that humans are used to.

Move away from that. Move higher in vibration. With the mind, go back, go forward to Montgomery Bell land, smooth, clear lake with geese all around. Music.

Open the heart link to Eagle and others who attended the Star Knowledge Conference.

When the world gets rough, think of the International Day of Peace, of love, broadcast yesterday afternoon. Think of the love of the gathering at the Star Knowledge Conference itself. All barriers down. Hearts open to receive love, light and peace to overlay the planet.

You have been with ancestors, angels, mound builders, dreamers, Brothers and Sisters. All were gathered -- little people, orbs, lights. All were there. All are here. A ship makes the heart above you. The waters danced. The stones recorded and held the records to overlay with Peace. The Peace Vibration was sent to the planet this day.

After this channeling, I receive another:

This one comes from our Sun.

My greetings and love this day of balance. May all be full of life and full of joy. I work ceaselessly to bring and sustain and grow life on all the planets of my Solar System. All, even an ant, a flea, a microbe receive my healing, growth, life energy. The trees stand to receive my Light. The plants artistically and strategically arrange their forms to receive the maximum exposure to my Light. The animals and humans and all living creatures absorb my light, bask in my Light. The Sea Creatures receive my Light. All stones and rock layers receive and hold my Light over millennia. Eternal Sun. Eternal Earth. Yes, there was a beginning for me. Yes, an end, but trillions and trillions of years in between. Bless each day with the turning of Mother Earth to my face. Today at the Equinox is her peak day of Balance -- up and down – Balance, Balance. The changing of the seasons in the Northern Hemisphere and the Southern Hemisphere. Rejoice in the Day. Rejoice in the Light. She is my Beloved Mother Earth and you are one of her inhabitants.

For the people of Mother Earth, be grateful. Give thanks to your Mother Earth who graciously offers you a ride through space. Enjoy your ride through space and the dimensions. The more Love, the more Light. The lighter you are, the more density falls off and Love expands so that Peace Prevails on Earth, so that Peace Prevails in Space and in all the planetary and universe systems.

Attend the planet. Attend all living forms. Cherish the waters and the ocean, their life forces. Cherish the air and the wind, their life forces.

Cherish the land and the fire, their life forces. Cherish the message of Love from all living beings. That is the frequency to broadcast through the planet, through space.

You have the Vortexes, the Frequency adjusters and amplifiers. You have the Sun Discs, the Frequency adjusters and amplifiers. You have the Crystals, the Frequency adjusters, amplifiers and record keepers. The Stones and Crystals hold my messages through the ages.

Beloved ones, my children on Earth, do not look to each other but up to see the gifts from me each day showering onto Mother Earth.

There is a time to rest, a time to play, a time to work, a time to gather and be thankful.

Being thankful is the whole meaning of the conference called The Great Thanksgiving.

Father Sun.

Note: I want to comment here that September 21 is traditionally called the Equinox, but this year, the Equinox is on September 22. Never mind. The Equinox is the Equinox. Same concept. Balance.

When we leave Nashville, a plane takes us to Newark where we wait two hours for another flight. The setting Sun is intense. Love spreads over the country. A golden Sun Dog, a rainbow is visible. A sign of success!!

On my second flight, I sit at the window facing the sunset and I look directly at the Sun. It is spinning, flashing white, red and green Light. A Whirling Sun. Equinox balance. Powerful Sun!!

CHAPTER 10

NIAGARA FALLS

Joint Journals:

September 26, Barbara Journal:

Everyone is invited to attend the September 27 and 28 Niagara Falls gathering called the EcoSpirit Native American Environmental Conference. Emphasis will be on the need for humanity, caretakers of Mother Earth, to step up and clean the environment for pure air to breathe, clean water to drink and nutritious food to eat.

Margaret and I feel this is a significant conference to attend and so, after 9:00 a.m. this morning, with Margaret driving, we leave for Niagara Falls. We have booked accommodations nearly across the street from the conference site and on arrival we will go to the hotel to park our car in the hotel's parking lot where it will stay until we leave Niagara Falls. What a convenience to stay at a hotel so close to the conference site! It eliminates transportation headaches.

Our route to Niagara Falls is via back roads unfamiliar to both of us but which Margaret prefers rather than driving on the fast Thruway. I hold Google maps in my hands to direct her as we enter unfamiliar territory, and I must say, the scenery is fun to watch. Nothing spectacular, but interesting. We see houses built a long time ago, trees living a long time, and then a McDonald's pops up and we realize that present tastes agree with those who seem to be living comfortably with the past.

Now, something strange happens. We are on Route 31 going West when a road to our left appears and seems to be the road we should take. So we do, because it too is going West. Then, when we see a road sign indicating we are about to enter a town, we do not see the town. Where is it? Never mind, we are traveling West, a direction that is of uppermost importance.

We think we are approaching the Iroquois National Wildlife Refuge and that would be interesting to see. But, we do not see any sign for a turnoff to this place. We shrug our shoulders. Then we see a sign saying we are approaching Royalton Corners and we reach it! Only a few miles further and we will be reaching Lockport whose quite recent history interests us. When the Erie Canal was being built so that merchandise could more easily move back and forth between the East and the West, the area that is now Lockport had to be part of the canal. However, when the Erie Canal crew reached this place, they had a big problem. The land lifted sharply. Meaning, locks needed to be built. But, the land lifted so sharply, five locks would be needed, one on top of the other! Who knew how to build like that? Well, it was figured out and the canal-building continued until it reached its destination, Lake Erie.

Margaret and I mention this place called Lockport in an earlier book, 2013 and Beyond, and now, 2014, it is fun cruising through this town thinking about the five locks built one on top of the other.

Soon we will reach Niagara Falls, and then the Google maps must serve us in a satisfactory manner. Also, we need to spot road signs, and here is where we have a problem. We see a sign for Route 14 and Margaret thinks we need to turn left. I think we need to keep straight ahead. Who is right? We are in traffic and there is not time to pause.

Well, straight ahead or left turn, we reach our hotel anyway. It is just before 12 noon, early for a check-in, but the receptionists at the front desk give us accommodations anyway. The hotel parking lot is packed with cars, but we find a space. Here, the car will sit until we leave in three days.

Now that we have reached our destination, we have an important task to do. Here is the background. About fifty years ago, Japanese shaman Master Goi visited Niagara Falls where he unexpectedly met a huge spiritual dragon deity, guardian of the North American continent. Because the karma of the continent was dark, the coat of the dragon had turned from white to black. Master Goi purified the coat to remove dark energies, and when this was done, the dragon's coat again became white.

We know this before going to Niagara Falls, and we understand the dragon's coat is again black. This needs to be changed to white, and that is our job. We will do our best.

For our work we will take a boat to the falls itself. This boat is called the Maid of the Mist. Our hotel is relatively close to the launching area, and we walk across a green park to reach the ticket booth and buy tickets. I see a boat has arrived with passengers wearing blue raincoats and I know they have just come from the falls. When they are off the boat, we, wearing blue raincoats, board and climb the stairs to the upper deck to stand at a guardrail ready to see the falls.

I do not know how many are on this boat, but it is full, and I think most boats taking this twenty-minute ride are full. Spectators from all over the world come here to take these boats to see the falls.

When we are ready to leave, a signal is sounded, and we wait expectantly for the first part of our boat adventure. Within a couple minutes, our boat has moved inside falls and water is blasting at us. Screams of joy! Our raincoats are doing their job of keeping us relatively dry. I am happy the weather is good. Even though it is the end of September, it is not cold.

When we enter these falls, Margaret and I begin working on turning the dragon's coat from black to white. We 'wash' it with the mighty blasts of water. We are happy the boat remains here while we are doing this work.

Now we move slowly to the main attraction -- massive falls. Our boat captain strategically moves us into this massive falls and then he stops the boat so we can have a wonderful experience of being massively drowned. What an experience! I can well understand why thousands come here every year from across the world to appreciate this unique place on the planet.

I have been speaking to the dragon, telling him we are cleaning his coat. Yes! I am focusing on this cleaning of the dragon's coat because the ultimate color will show the balance of the North American continent. Well, getting the balance is better said than done!

We stay here a long time, and then the boat begins to slowly return to its dock to unload us and take on other passengers. On arrival, I stay at my place at the railing, waiting for most to leave. The boat's captain, wearing a starched white business shirt, is also ready to leave the boat and he comes near me. I do not see a drop of water on him and I cannot resist pointing this out. He tells me that if he had to be soaked day in and day out every day, he would not be on the boat. Well, I can understand that. For him, it's just a job. For me, my work today is all-important here.

When Margaret and I leave the boat, we put our blue raincoats in a recycle bin, and then we walk to the river of water where it goes sharply downward at the first falls where our boat had stopped. Yes, the water is coming fast, but where the land and the water meet, before the water goes downward, the water is somewhat calm because of the configuration of the uneven land here. I am thinking that if a person is unexpectedly caught in the water, here is a place where he has a bit of a chance to get out, especially if people on land are trying to save him.

September 27:

When the EcoSpirit Native American Environmental Conference begins at 8 a.m., I am thinking this is an early hour to begin a conference. Will most people stay away until later? No. I soon realize most are here because probably they want to hear the opening speaker, Paul Dyster, Mayor of Niagara Falls. He speaks only a short time, but he is an adventure to listen to. He is mature, articulate and to the point. Later, I learn he had been a college professor. Hence, a practiced speaker. Also, he was the president of this board and that board and an arms control negotiator for the State Department in Geneva, Switzerland. On and on his references go. I think maybe some day he may decide to expand by running for President of the U.S.A.

Another speaker is Uqualla, a Medicine Man from the Havasupai tribe of the Grand Canyon whom I met a couple years ago. I listen to him speaking slowly and with articulation to explain that 'we are all the same' and we can look within to our hearts for the growing of Beauty and Love and Peace.

Clifford Mahooty, a member of the Zuni Pueblo Indian Tribe of New Mexico, speaks at the Nashville conference and it is good to see him again. His passion is to spread understanding among people, and, to do this, he travels extensively throughout the country. He is an environmentalist who knows what needs to be done to clean the air, the water and the land. He says the people are slow to listen.

For the first time I meet Michael Bastine, an Algonquin healer and wise man who has written a book with Mason Winfield, Iroquois Supernatural: Talking Animals and Medicine People. He is an excellent speaker whose focus is on sparking the heart of humanity to recognize the energies of Nature so that the energies of Nature can be united with the energies of humanity when solving environmental problems. Of great interest to me is that he believes all humanity is good. If there is conflict, it is a conflict between the heart and the ego. He says that youth need to be taught to be good humans, to honor Nature, to honor all that makes up our world.

September 28:

Native American tradition is that sunrise be honored, and we are asked to attend a ceremony this morning at 6:15 on Goat Island at

Terrapin Point. Fortunately, yesterday at the conference we meet two women staying at our hotel who will drive us to this event. Goat Island is not far, but, Terrapin Point? Where is that? We are given instructions, and we actually drive to Goat Island with no difficulty, but, where is Terrapin Point?

We creep along not knowing where we are going and now a car is coming behind us, driven by a conference member living close to Niagara Falls. She knows exactly where to go and we follow her, park when she parks, and then we walk with her as she goes downhill to Terrapin Point which we realize overlooks the falls.

The sky is blue and the sun is coming up bright red. Margaret and I are thinking about the dragon we have changed from black to white. Because Niagara Falls is the home of this guardian, with our minds, we will make Terrapin Point the center point of his home. This morning's ceremony will strengthen what needs to be done -- a cleaning of the continent, a wiping way of negativity and the placing of Peace, Love, and Light onto the land. Balance. That is what Mother Earth needs on this continent, and what she needs throughout the world.

When others arrive just before the sun 'wakens' for the day, a sacred Native American pipe ceremony begins.

_____

_____

Margaret Journal:

September 26:

I am up at 2:30 a.m., too excited to sleep. Tomorrow I will be going to Niagara Falls to attend a two-day EcoSpirit Native American Environmental Conference. I pack at 5:00 a.m., have breakfast, and I am ready to drive to Niagara Falls at 8:00 a.m. It is a bright and beautiful day as I slowly drive through farmlands of corn and cabbage. The foliage is putting on fall colors.

We arrive at Niagara Falls at 10:30 a.m., take a room at the Sheraton Hotel, settle our bags, and leave at 11:11 a.m. (Mother Earth time) to walk to the Maid of the Mist boat launch. We reach it by walking through a park and we are soon joining many crowds of people from all over the world -- Chinese, Pakistanis, Indians, Europeans -- all cheerful people going to the falls.

Our reason for coming to the falls today is to see the guardian of the North American continent, a black dragon that was originally white. In the early1970's, Japanese Master Goi returned the color to white. He said the negative actions of the people had changed the color. We are coming to the falls to give love to the dragon, to wash out dark frequencies in the turmoil of the pounding, roaring water.

When we take the elevator down to the Maid of the Mist boat, the elevator man is full of sweetness and jokes. All the staff are enthusiastically greeting the visitors, welcoming them to a grand journey into the falls.

When we reach the boat, we climb aboard to stand on the second level at the railing on the left because we think this will be a good spot for working with the falls. We leave at 12:12 p.m. (a sacred time for change), and we are soon under the drenching spray of the falls.

I conceive of the Great Spirit Dragon being cleaned by the water cascading down. The water sprays up to form a great vortex of energy.

Now the boat journeys to Horseshoe Falls where the falls envelope the boat with drenching water and wind. I look at the falls on the left and I look at the falls on the right. All is churning water. I am totally soaked. It is a breath-taking moment to be in the middle of tons of water cascading down.

As the boat begins to turn away, in the mist at the base of the falls, I see a shimmering rainbow. A Rainbow of Peace! A rainbow making the dragon all colors. A moment of transformation!

On the way back to the dock I see cormorants fishing and some sunning themselves on a large rock. At the dock we slowly disembark to walk up the hill to the elevators, discarding along the way in recycle bins our blue rain gear with the large 'Maid of the Mist' logo on the front.

We walk to a high tower overlooking the falls. A majestic view! Then we walk down to see the rushing water plunging over the edge. I celebrate our work with the Spirit Dragon here.

Now we walk along the river and through the park to return to our hotel. In the room I write up my notes, focusing on the boat adventure and the dragon. I place the Vortexes at the window. We are here at the mighty power center for the North American continent. We are at the Mighty Ridge! The Niagara Escarpment! The sacred Musical Rapture is playing and I know the Dolphins and Angels have come to be with us. We bask in this amazing day!

September 27:

We walk across the street to the Niagara Falls Conference Center to attend the EcoSpirit Native American Environmental Conference. It begins early, 8:00 a.m., with a welcoming speech by the Mayor of Niagara Falls, Paul Dyster. He is an enthusiastic, compassionate man who is a strong advocate for environmental and community relations. I find him to be excellent, a person who really cares. While he is speaking, I feel the presence of Nature Spirits who want their voices heard to save the environment--the bears, eagles, dolphins, whales. Many spirits. Also, the devas of the flowers and trees. The auditorium is full of them.

Speaker Zuni Elder Clifford Mahooty tells us that people must return to the early knowledge of working with Mother Earth and not against her. Education is the key, he says. As an engineer, he has seen the disconnect in the modern approach to the environment that has caused long-term damage. Listen to the old people, he says. The native people who know the natural ways. He has seen the problems from all sides. He works tirelessly to educate people on the need to change laws so that further damage to the land, air and water is stopped. Too much damage has happened during his lifetime.

Speaker Uqualla of the Havasupai Tribe from the Grand Canyon speaks and he says one must honor Mother Nature and one must learn how to speak to Spirit, how to be in the presence of Awe. While he is speaking, I feel powerful energies of both the Grand Canyon and Niagara Falls.

A presentation given by Allan Jamieson II on herbs tells how to find herbs, harvest them, care for them, and use them for medicinal purposes. I am excited to hear his knowledge that stems from the Native American culture. Later, we go to a workshop to learn more.

This has been an amazing day with native and non-native people having the same mindset. Organizer Bill Tenuto tells me there will be another environmental conference next year.

September 28:

Today, Mike Bastine, an Algonquin Elder, speaks about peace and balance, and he stresses the importance of women in the Iroquois society. He points out there should be balance between male and female, and he says there is an innate balance in Nature that is honored by the Native American. Mike says one must live life with love, kindness and compassion. We have been given beautiful gifts from the universe. We must stand up and take care of Mother Earth and everything living on her.

Speaker John Volpe, Algonquin Elder, says the animals in the water -- the fish, the turtles, the frogs -- are his people and we must have respect for his family. He is deeply concerned about the contamination of the waters. Many living in the water have become diseased and some can no longer reproduce their young. Their distress is a warning sign to humans, like the canary in a mine. He wants the environment cleaned of manmade toxins. Damaging factors affect both humans and animals. We are all one.

September 28, Sunday:

Before listening to the speakers today, early in the morning we leave the hotel to go to a sunrise tobacco and pipe ceremony at Terrapin Point on Goat Island. Two conference ladies, a mother and daughter, offer to drive us. We reach the island easily but we do not know how to reach Terrapin Point. A Canadian living near Niagara Falls who is attending the conference arrives in her car and we follow her. I feel the pull of the river close by but it is still dark, too dark to see.

When it becomes lighter, we walk to Terrapin Point. It is misty. Sea gulls are walking and then slowly circling in the sky after their night's sleep. They are not bothered by us. They feel our compatibility with them and the river flowing, the falls sounding, the power of the whole force field. The sky begins turning from soft light to bright. The mist becomes red.

We form a circle for the pipe ceremony, smudging and saying prayers. Drumming begins and powerful singing. A man wearing a Scottish jacket points out a faint outline of a rainbow appearing near the falls. The rainbow became brighter and brighter, clearer and clearer, so that the full arch of the rainbow is visible before us, reaching from the US side to the Canadian side of the falls. The rainbow stays throughout. What a blessing to see it. It is amazing to be here at sunrise at Goat Island!

September 29:

Margaret Channeling:

1:30 a.m., I speak to the White Dragon and I say the EcoSpirit conference is a success. It has brought key people together to begin the process of listening to Mother Earth and addressing environmental damage to air, water, land and fire. I ask the Spirit Dragon to please comment.

Response: Yes, I see you cannot sleep. Too much to think about. Too much to ponder. Your mind cannot comprehend so vast a complexity. Time moves forward as the river flows over the falls with great force that gives energy to this place to meet. The power of the water speaks to the hearts of those who come to see the splendor of the immensity of the falls. Awe-inspiring energy given to the core of humanity. Creator Source, Creation beginning, moving forward over eons of time. All of this is comprehended in the presence of the falls. Like the waterfall, this represents new beginnings as the water approaches and races over the Niagara ridge to crash below and move onward and outward to the Atlantic Ocean.

Niagara Falls is the sacred water center of the world, a power generator of the Spirit. This is why it is a good idea to gather here.

You are thinking about the next EcoSpirit conference that can map the strategy to reverse ecological damage concerning the key issues of water viability, reduction of sunlight, quality of air, change in the climate, continuing shift in tectonic plates. The key is to include the younger generation to start rowing and to not continue to sit back asleep in the boat of Life. In one's own way, each person contributes his/her own talent.

A league of friends -- this is what bonds the group of planners for next year. The glue that holds it together is the Love of Mother Earth. The momentum is Spirit. Pick topics and move forward like Allan the herbalist who investigates three new herbs per year. Pick three lines to follow for next year. Tell the people about this in the in same manner as a drumbeat calling everyone to gather. Use word of mouth and the Internet. Do a Facebook page of pictures and also create a newsletter to report high points of the meeting.

Gather the flowers. Make a bouquet. Send it out as a force field on the horizon. The mighty rainbow came out and sealed the approval of the correct action. Spirit weaves the course. There is a force that cannot be stopped. Like the water, it moves. The animals, the fish, the dolphins, the bears, the birds filled up the chairs in the conference meeting room. They attended, endorsed, and cheered on the effort. Go forward. Do not drop the ball or let your spirit flag. Keep the focus narrow. Organize the course of action for next year. Spread the word. The world of Spirit is behind you. Mother Earth is for you. Harmony and unity, the force field of the Niagara Escarpment is behind you. We are here, the Brothers and Sisters of the Vortexes, Higher Worlds, dolphins and whales, and the Dragon of water power, essence. White. All colors in one. White.

Now sleep, dear Margaret. You have a spirit knot in your stomach. Rest. There is a time to work and a time to rest.

After writing the channeling, in my mind's eye I see unfolding a large symbol, Spiritual Law of Choice. This is very appropriate on all levels.

September 29:

I wake early in the morning when it is still dark. As the dawn light comes, the day starts foggy. What a joy that yesterday was such a bright, beautiful day. We easily pack and check out and we are on the road by 9:00 a.m.

In the afternoon, high in the sky, I think I see powerful space ships in the forms of clouds. Many welcoming us back. The sun is bright now. I feel love from the sun.

In the late afternoon, I speak with my Native American friend SilverStar and she says the rainbow is a sign of Creator's love.

The trip to Niagara Falls has been awesome! A gift. A blessing.

CHAPTER 11

LOVELAND, COLORADO STAR KNOWLEDGE CONFERENCE

Joint Journals:

November 9, Barbara Journal:

Native American Chief Golden Light Eagle has invited us to speak at his Colorado Star Knowledge Conference, November 10-12, at Sunrise Retreat Center in Loveland, Colorado, about seventy miles from Denver.

United Airlines takes Margaret and me to Denver via Chicago, and along the way, we listen to TV weather reports for the next few days. Snow, snow and more snow. Record breaking temperatures. The huge Polar Vortex that resides in the Arctic has moved South with an intention of taking up residence in the U.S.A. Does it have a passport?

Fortunately, we are given predictions earlier and so we dress warmly -- winter boots and all. When we arrive at the Denver Airport, it is pleasantly warm, although we know the weather will be changing, and it does change! The first day of the conference, we look out the windows and snow is coming down. Not a heavy snow, but nevertheless snow, and it has no intention of stopping.

We think of the one hundred plus elk in a nearby pasture greeting us. The first night they call all night, but when the snow begins they stop. I think of them standing in the cold with the snow landing on them. They have no place to go to avoid such weather. How fortunate we two-leggeds are!

September 10:

Our scheduled talk is on the second day, November 11, a special day for Mother Earth on the Native American calendar, and we are pleased that our talk will be on that special day. But, in this world, we are used to fluidity, and yes, on Day One of the conference, November 10, we meet fluidity face on. The third speaker has not arrived. His car and an elk have met while he was driving to the conference, and so, both the elk and his car can go nowhere.

Margaret and I are asked to push up our talk by one day, and we agree. We will be speaking on carrying around the world Vortexes of energy to help heal the world. The information had been given to Chief Golden Light Eagle telepathically by Star Elders over a long period of time, and he has agreed for us to send out the information. This book in your hands. plus our books, 2013 And Beyond and 2013 And Beyond Part II, include these journeys.

What are these Vortexes? Powerful energy fields presented to the world of humanity so they can be used to help solve problems. For example, they can be used to lift the heavy weight of negativity off an area that has been struck by wars begun by differences among humanity. Also, where there is a weakness in Mother Earth's plate structure, such as the structure between the two continents of South America and Africa, powerful positive energy of the Vortexes can be laid down to counter the weakness. Even the path of a typhoon can be altered by using the energy of the Vortexes.

Yes, there are many ways to use these energies to help Mother Earth and all living on Her. She is a vast entity, and so traveling everywhere to help would be difficult. Yet, it is not essential to go everywhere to help because what is being given, energy, is being used by the mind. Thoughts have no attached mileage. It is a matter of directing thought.

_____

_____

The remainder of the chapter is from Margaret's Journal.

November 9:

How amazing! We have first class tickets to Chicago. The dolphins say it was arranged by the Admirals of the Sky, the whales and the dolphins.

In Chicago, we learn our flight to Denver is cancelled. Where can we go to book another flight? A passenger with her boyfriend helps us find a big flight board and then Customer Service where a kind attendant books another flight for us to Denver.

We wait at the gate and see people in long lines rebooking their flights. We watch this while sitting next to a Canadian couple with their little daughter who frowns and smiles and waves and eats oatmeal patiently being offered by her mother.

Our flight to Denver is packed. We sit far to the back, I at the window and Barbara in the middle seat. The aisle seat is for a stewardess who is flying West to do a red-eye flight back to Washington, D.C.

After landing at the Denver Airport, we need to find a Super Shuttle van to take us seventy miles to the conference center at Sunrise Ranch in Loveland, Colorado. A Hospitality Ambassador wearing a big smile and a white cowboy hat helps us find our exit door to the shuttles and busses. We know we need to wait almost an hour for our shuttle, and so we sit inside the terminal and speak with a 73-year-old woman from Ohio who travels the world. She has just visited the Ukraine, Russia, Poland, Slovenia, etc. Next year, with her husband, she plans to take a boat trip in Holland and then travel to St. Petersburg.

When it is time to board the shuttle to travel North to the Sunrise Ranch at Loveland, I look at the distant, magnificent Rocky Mountains. The Great Divide. As we leave the airport area, I look back at the great white tents (sails), part of the airport entrance, echoing the mountains. I watch the lenticular clouds above us. One great cloud is over our van. Could this be a space ship? I see sets of stacked clouds over one section of the mountains. Is this a landing base for our Brothers and Sisters?

We are on our way to Love Land, spelled Loveland, pronounced 'Lovelun' with an emphasis on the first syllable. I still like saying that we are going to <u>Love</u> <u>Land</u>. Before arriving at Sunrise Ranch, we change to a smaller van driven by a woman originally from California who tells us about low humidity here that can cause very dry skin, nose problems, etc. When we arrive at Sunrise Ranch, we are given a room across the street from the conference building, and then I walk a bit to see the lake in the distance. Later, when elk are bugling, there is a need to see them, too. Between one hundred and two hundred and they talk all night.

I am deeply grateful to be here. I feel I am with my star family that has been assembled here. I channel anyone who wishes to speak.

The Pleiadians answer: Yes, you need to come aboard. Pick any key and enter. The entryway is through the heart. That is why there is a need to have silence and to be silent. Speaking heart to heart. The frequency of contact is through intent. We are all working for peace for Mother Earth, for strength, for recognition of what she is doing – allowing a stage for Life to be enacted upon.

We are here to temper the energies, to protect, to shield, to balance. To encourage right living on Earth. To be in harmony, to spread the peace of love intent vibration that you see in the great meeting room at Sunrise Ranch.

We are here. You picked up the vibration. You are here to help heal the planet. Mother Earth welcomes you. We welcome you and this group that gathers here. Drill wells of knowledge and compassion and appreciation for Mother Earth.

You think you did not bring an offering, but you brought the Vortex Symbols containing the reflection of the Divine and the high standards of living at peace inter-galactically -- space – universes – galaxies. All is alive and well.

The heart is a link to the floors of understanding of different realities.

Your concern is for Peace. May Peace Prevail on Earth. Your concern is for the environment – that the planet is 'not consumed' to the detriment of the planet.

Peace, Sustainability, Thriving, Gratitude, Thanksgiving. Balance in Action, Consideration of Consequences, Protection of Nature.

Next to these words, I draw the symbols of Universal Law of Movement and Balance, Spiritual Growth of Man, Spiritual Law of Choice, Spiritual Law of Future Sight, and Spiritual Law of Protection (of Nature).

The channeling continues: *Everything exists at the same time. We enjoy being here, right here in this room -- or, are you here with us in our room?*

Since we are one, we have the same frequency channels. For Vortex, dial 101. For the sacred number of Mother Earth, dial 1111. All channels reach the same source.

Come. Come. Come. Let us attend the conference together.

November 10:

An amazing day!

I decide to walk outside to the morning sunrise. The sun is bright, crystalline, calling me to walk to it as it rises. The day is bright. People are coming back from seeing the elk. I walk on the main road and then turn right to go up a dirt drive to the crest of a ridge. I stand looking at the herd far off in the distance. I give love and greetings to the elk at sunrise. I then return to look at the sun and the lake. All is in perfection. I take a mental photo of this peace on Earth. The Elk is the guardian of the Spiritual Law of Protection and when combined with the Universal Law of Nature, this forms the Vortex of True Nature. I spread the image over the world. Peace and Harmony from Loveland, Sunrise Ranch.

The conference opening ceremony begins at 8:00 a.m. with drummers gathering to drum and sing. The first speaker is Jennifer Marks who does an excellent power point presentation on the Arcturians and their wisdom (galactic). Then Chief Golden Light Eagle says Barbara and I are to speak now because the next speaker, shaman Mazatzin, has had a car accident. He and an elk clashed on the highway. Barbara says this is an elk giveaway.

I rush to bring our speaking notes and Vortexes. Then, with Barbara holding Vortex illustrations for the audience, I begin explaining the Vortex meanings. Unexpectedly, SilverStar puts the entire Vortex Complex on a large screen and shows the symbols as we speak. What a surprise she has given us!

Because our speech is unexpected and we must give it spontaneously, we use a carefree, 'let it rip' type of humor. When a page is dropped we tell the audience it is a 'technical malfunction'. I point to Barbara and she points to me. The audience laughs and has a good time. We relax and have a good time. Many come afterwards to tell us they liked our talk.

At noon, we have lunch with a Japanese young man who was with us at Mount Fuji, Japan, when a typhoon hit and a lenticular cloud cap appeared at the top of the mountain. When it descended it became the dragon ring around the mountain. We are told this is the moment when all could be healed if touched by Ainu shaman Grandmother Rera who is with us. Gold could be seen coming out of her hands. This memory will remain with us forever.

As for now, we are far from Japan, in the mountains of Colorado and it begins to snow. We have been expecting this.

November 11:

6:50 a.m. we awake to dress warmly and go across the road to a sunrise ceremony conducted by shaman Mazatzin who will be honoring his son born 11:11 and recently killed. When the ceremony ends, all of us are asked to speak a blessing. I say, May the love of Loveland be spread around the world on this special day, 11:11.

Later this morning, I listen to Mazatzin speak about the ancient calendar. He tells us today is the day of the serpent on the Aztec calendar. I know today is the Universal Law of Judgment on the Star Knowledge calendar with the Earth guardian as the snake. I think, wouldn't it be interesting to compare the two calendars day by day to see the overlapping and to discover that the two calendar systems come from the same source? Are they interlinked? Yes, this calendar project would be a great research project for someone connected to both systems.

When Chief Golden Light Eagle begins his speech, he explains that the first channeling received from the Higher Worlds was the Universal Law of Free Will. He points out that November 11 is during the time of Remembrance, and that is why we are all here.

During Grandma Chandra's session, we do a meditation for healing. I focus on the healing of the Pacific waters. I also feel that the golden energies of the Rocky Mountains are love frequencies. I see the mountains as white pyramids echoing the Universal Law of Light, Sound and Vibration Symbols transformed into golden hearts of love. For the radiation, I see a rise in the dimensions -- higher and higher frequencies. Then I see vertical shafts of code symbols descending from the Higher Worlds to clear the water of the Pacific. The meditation ends with the high rose flower frequency.

I take a workshop with Annette Price who focuses on the dignity and care of horses. She is dedicated to raising the consciousness of humanity concerning the treatment of animals. Horses are healers and teachers, she says. During the workshop, Annette has a deck of horse cards and she says we each can have one of them, but we must shuffle the deck to choose one. I watch as each person shuffles the deck and picks a card. When it is my turn, I shuffle and pick one and it is the Arabian horse reminding me of the white horse I loved in Qatar.

Now we go into meditation and I feel/see the wild horses of the West. They are running off in the distance. Then the Arabians come in close and one stands behind me. At the end of the meditation, a golden horse appears and says, Come aboard for a ride, and off we go.

November 12:

In the early morning, I write in my journal: There is a feeling of completeness at Loveland conference. Spiritual people are here. Healers. Ego-less. The elk are close by. The mountains are close by. The magpie attended yesterday's sunrise ceremony. The horse frequency is here. The Brothers and Sisters are here in the softness of the snow. A delightful place to be – Sunrise Ranch.

When speaker Randy Hutton talks on the healing of the waters, I learn he was a commercial fisherman who saw the water pollution problem. He studied the nature of water and applied sacred geometry, crystals, and spiral forms to bring health and vitality to the water. Today he has formed his own company, Vibrant, Vital Water, and travels to teach how to revitalize water. During the morning, Chief Golden Light Eagle conducts a naming ceremony for a young girl attended by her grandmother. In Native American tradition, this is a special ceremony, and the chief considers carefully the name which will remain for a lifetime. He says the girl speaks with all animals, and for this reason, she will be given that name. He takes from his bonnet a special feather to put in her hair.

The last speaker of the conference is Patty Turner, founder of The Sacred Earth Foundation, who works to help the environment with shamans from indigenous communities around the world. She speaks about being a part of a sacred gathering in Greenland and people from all over the world, 150, come to be with her at a sacred fire.

Patty Turner tells about the importance of giving prayers and tobacco for healing. She explains that high above her home in Colorado is a flat stone which she likes to reach for meditation. Before meditating she always puts tobacco around the big stone. Eventually, she planted grass around it. At another place, she climbed to a tall oak tree and gave blessings. Then there was an intense wild fire where everything was burned. Afterwards, she climbed to the tall flat stone and she saw that the grass was still growing. When she climbed to see the oak tree, all the trees were burned and fallen expect the oak tree. She tells us that the power of prayer is very great.

Yes, the experience of going to the Colorado conference is a great one.

GLOSSARY

Sacred Music

MUSICAL RAPTURE, A Healing Gift for Humanity, can be downloaded via Patricia Cota-Robles' website, http://www. eraofpeace.org/musical-rapture

As her son Joao stated on his mother's website: "The frequency of this Celestial Music communicates with the Divine Intelligence of the body at a cellular level raising the consciousness of each cell. As the music soothes and comforts the cells, the body's natural ability to heal itself is enhanced."

Vortexes

Chief Golden Light Eagle and Grandmother SilverStar have given us valuable information on how to use powerful energy fields to help Mother Earth and all that live on her. This information has come from sacred ceremony and the information is in a booklet, The Vortexes, The Universal Symbols and Laws of Creation: *A Divine Plan by Which One Can Live.* The Heavenly Hosts, The Servants of Creator. Copyright 2013 Revised Edition.

To order, click on http://www.starelders.net/Books_Calendar.html

There are illustrations of Symbols and fuller explanation in the book, Maka Wicahpi Wicohan: Universal and Spiritual Laws of Creator.

Star Law Manual of the Galactic Federation. Copyright 1996 by
Standing Elk.

There are eleven Vortex Symbols, each formed by a joining of one
Universal Law with one Spiritual Law.

The **Vortex of Light, Sound and Vibration** is formed by joining the
Universal Law of Light, Sound and Vibration with the Spiritual Law
of Intuition. As an aside, one has to use one's own intuitive mind to
achieve the understanding that goes back to the origins of the planet
where there was the original sound and light vibration of creation.

The **Vortex of Integrity** is formed by the Universal Law of Free Will
combining with the Spiritual Freedom of Man. This is a free will
planet and can only operate fully when there is complete spiritual
freedom of man. There should be freedom with truth and honesty.

The **Vortex of Symmetry** is formed by combining the Universal Law
of Symmetry with the Spiritual Law of Equality. Symmetry means
balance between all things, both spiritual and material. As above,
so below. Also, equality between male/female, left/right brain, etc.

The **Vortex of Strength, Health and Happiness** is formed with
the combining of the Universal Law of Movement and Balance
with Spiritual Strength, Health and Happiness. In life one has to
be balanced to move forward and also one has to move forward to
be balanced. Balance is symmetry in motion. With movement and
balance come strength and health and happiness.

The **Vortex of Right Relationship** is produced by combining
the Universal Law of Innocence, Truth and Family with Spiritual
Protection of Family. This is also a powerful Vortex of social
relationship (based on truth) when the concept has moved from the
individual to the group.

The **Vortex of Growth** is formed when the Universal Law of Change
is combined with the Spiritual Growth of Man. Change is a basic
tenant of life. With spiritual growth, all things thrive. All things
change. Nothing is static. Therefore, both the individual and society

need the spiritual growth of man. When humanity grows spiritually, then the Vortex of Growth flourishes. In the natural state, all things grow unhindered. With spiritual growth all things thrive.

The **Vortex of True Judgment** is formed by combining the Universal Law of Judgment with the Spiritual Law of Karma. All actions should be looked at through the eyes of the Universal Law of Judgment so that no harm is done and there is no karma. The latter, the consequences of action, can be turned into darma, teaching. This law applies socially as well as environmentally.

The **Vortex of Perception** is formed by the combining of the Universal Law of Perception combined with the Spiritual Law of Future Sight. It is important to perceive the impact of one's actions and to use the gift of future sight. Needed now are planetary actions that affect in a good way the lives of the people in relationship to the air, the water, the land, the life on this planet.

The **Vortex of Connection to Life** is formed with the combining of the Universal Law of Life with the Spiritual Law of Choice. Life is enhanced by correct choices. It is diminished by poor choices. Therefore, choose wisely. Choice and Life are integrally connected.

The **Vortex of True Nature** is formed by the combining of the Universal Law of Nature with the Spiritual Law of Protection. Nature exists and thrives. It is up to mankind to protect Nature so that all life thrives on this planet.

The **Vortex of Love** is formed by combining the Universal Law of Love with the Spiritual Law of Healing. One has to have Love to give healing and to receive healing. Love is the greatest healer. People, Nature, all creatures, plants, cells, molecules, atoms, adamantine particles respond to Love. All have a consciousness. Love creates. Love heals. Love is the highest power of all.

When the Vortexes are displayed in a circle, the center point is called **Universal Unity and Spiritual Integrity**. All Vortexes bring unity. All Vortexes thrive with integrity. Integrity is the foundation of the Vortexes.

Calendar Set

To order the calendar set called MAKA WICAHPI WICOHAN WANIYETU, The Universal Symbols and Laws of Laws of Creation in Day by Day Living, click on http://www.starelders.net